FOUL DEEDS IN
KENSINGTON AND CHELSEA

TRUE CRIME FROM WHARNCLIFFE
Foul Deeds and Suspicious Deaths Series

OTHER TRUE CRIME BOOKS FROM WHARNCLIFFE

Please contact us via any of the methods below for more information or a catalogue
WHARNCLIFFE BOOKS
47 Church Street, Barnsley, South Yorkshire, S70 2AS
Tel: 01226 734555 • 734222 • Fax: 01226 734438
email: enquiries@pen-and-sword.co.uk
website: www.wharncliffebooks.co.uk

Foul Deeds in
KENSINGTON
& CHELSEA

John J Eddleston

First Published in Great Britain in 2010 by
Wharncliffe Local History
an imprint of
Pen and Sword Books Limited,
47 Church Street, Barnsley,
South Yorkshire. S70 2AS

Copyright © John J Eddleston, 2010

ISBN: 978 184563 128 4

The right of John J Eddleston to be identified as
author of this work has been asserted by him
in accordance with the Copyright, Designs and Patents Act, 1988.

A CIP catalogue record of this book is available from the
British Library.

Typeset in Plantin and Benguiat by
S L Menzies-Earl

Printed in the UK by the MPG Books Group

Pen & Sword Books Ltd incorporates the imprints of
Pen & Sword Aviation, Pen & Sword Maritime,
Pen & Sword Military, Wharncliffe Local History, Pen & Sword Select,
Pen & Sword Military Classics, Leo Cooper, Remember When, Seaforth
Publishing and Frontline Publishing

For a complete list of Pen & Sword titles please contact:
PEN & SWORD BOOKS LIMITED
47 Church Street, Barnsley, South Yorkshire, S70 2AS, England.
E-mail: enquiries@pen-and-sword.co.uk
Website: www.pen-and-sword.co.uk

Contents

Introduction

The upmarket areas of Kensington and Chelsea have seen some fascinating stories, from the darker side of life.

Amongst the most famous cases of all are those of John George Haigh, who claimed his first victims in the area, and Ronald True, the upper-class killer who managed to escape the noose, to a massive public outcry. There are, however, lesser known, but equally fascinating cases.

There is, for example, the murder of Catherine Elmes, a crime for which John Sharpe confessed, later withdrawing his statement, leaving the case unsolved; or the story of Joseph O'Sullivan and Reginald Dunne, who committed a political assassination; or Dennis Muldowney, a man who took the life of a war heroine.

The area set some unique records in the field of true crime. Kenneth Gilbert and Ian Grant, for example, killed in the area and were the last men ever hanged at the same establishment, at the same time, for the same crime. Then there is Guenther Podola, the last man ever hanged for the murder of a policeman.

These areas of London are, perhaps, amongst the most luxurious areas of the modern city, but those well-kept streets have much more sinister tales to tell.

I would like to offer my thanks to Yvonne, my wife, who assisted with the research for this volume, proof read every single chapter and supported me throughout. I would also like to thank the staff of The National Archives at Kew. It is always a pleasure to work there and without their assistance, the research for books such as this would be much more difficult.

Acknowledgements

All references are from The National Archives:

HO 64/3/130	Catherine Elmes	CRIM 1/1928	George Cyril Epton
CRIM 1/29/6	James White	DPP 2/1738	George Cyril Epton
CRIM 1/37/1	Owen Leonard	DPP 2/1755	George Cyril Epton
CRIM 1/37/6	John Noble	MEPO 3/3007	George Cyril Epton
CRIM 1/38/3	Walter Hosler	PCOM 8/2136	George Cyril Epton
HO 144/543/ A54575	Walter Hosler	CRIM 1/1836	Thomas John Ley and Lawrence John Smith
CRIM 1/41/4	Reginald Saunderson	DPP 2/1579	Ley and Smith
CRIM 1/108/7	Alice Jane Money	DPP 2/1609	Ley and Smith
CRIM 1/113/5	Madan Lal Dhingra	DPP 2/1840	John George Haigh
MEPO 3/2688	Frances Buxton	HO 45/23633	John George Haigh
CRIM 1/200/4	Ronald True	HO 45/23634	John George Haigh
DPP 1/71	Ronald True	MEPO 3/3128	John George Haigh
HO 45/25421	Ronald True	PCOM 9/818	John George Haigh
HO 144/2568	Ronald True	CRIM 1/2252	Dennis George Muldowney
MEPO 3/1572	Ronald True		
CRIM 1/748	George Frank Harvey	DPP 2/2169	Dennis George Muldowney
DPP 2/238	George Frank Harvey	PCOM 9/1634	Dennis George Muldowney
HO 144/19912	George Frank Harvey	CRIM 1/2428	Kenneth Gilbert & Ian Arthur Grant
HO 144/19913	George Frank Harvey	DPP 2/2336	Gilbert and Grant
		MEPO 2/9543	Gilbert and Grant
MEPO 3/1696	George Frank Harvey	CRIM 1/3246	Guenther Fritz Erwin Podola
DPP 2/900	Harold Dorian Trevor	DPP 2/2979	Guenther Podola
		HO 291/245	Guenther Podola
DPP 2/949	Harold Dorian Trevor	MEPO 2/9896	Guenther Podola
HO 144/21586	Harold Dorian Trevor	CRIM 1/4013	Marilyne Anne Bain
MEPO 3/2194	Harold Dorian Trevor	DPP 2/3535	Marilyne Anne Bain
PCOM 9/2099	Harold Dorian Trevor	CRIM 1/4885	Robert Lipman
		DPP 2/4443	Robert Lipman

Chapter 1

Francis Losch
1818

Francis Losch was a native of Luxembourg and, at the age of seventeen, had joined the Austrian Army. Having served his adopted country with credit, he then moved to England and joined the 3rd Battalion of the 60th Regiment of Foot, stationed in the West Indies. Finally, after many years of military service, he retired from the army, and married a much younger woman, Mary Ann, who went by the name of Nance. Losch then settled down at 7 Jew's Row, Sloane Street, as a Chelsea Pensioner.

On Friday, 9 October 1818, Ann Diamond, a widow, who lodged at the same house as the Loschs, saw them at the top of Lawrence's Yard. Mary Ann Losch was walking a few paces ahead of her husband, and as she approached Ann, Mary asked how she was. Ann replied that she was well and, unable to clearly see the man who was still approaching, asked Mary if it was her husband.

Even before Mary Ann could reply, Francis Losch stopped near the two women and said, 'Nance, you are drunk, come and go home.' Immediately, Mary Ann called back, 'If I am drunk, it is caused by prostituting myself to keep such an idle fellow as you.' There was no reply. Francis merely stepped forward, took something from beneath his coat and plunged it violently into Mary Ann's side.

Mary Ann staggered against Ann Diamond and then slowly fell to the ground. As she dropped, Mary Ann screamed out, 'Take the knife out of my body.' As Ann looked on in horror, Francis Losch calmly leaned back against a wall and said, 'Here I am, and anybody may take me that chooses.'

Various people came to Mary Ann's aid and she was rushed to

St George's Hospital. However, despite prompt medical attention, she died from her wound later that night and Francis found himself facing a charge of wilful murder.

The inquest opened before Mr Hugh Lewis, the coroner for Westminster, at the *Triumphant Chariot* public house in Grosvenor Place. Before any witnesses were called, the jury were first escorted to the hospital to view the body, and were then taken back to Grosvenor Place.

After Ann Diamond had given her testimony, Richard Clark was called to the stand. He stated that at approximately 8.00pm on 9 October, he had been in Lawrence's Yard and had seen the two ladies talking together. Richard heard Francis Losch say something, in a low voice, and then heard a scream as Mary Ann fell to the ground.

Richard Treadway was also in Lawrence's Yard and he heard Mary Ann shout, 'My God, I am murdered!' He saw her fall and ran to see if he could offer any assistance. Although it was quite dark, he could see that she had a very bad wound through which her bowels were protruding. Richard, with another man named George Carter, took Francis into custody and began to escort him to the local watchhouse. On the way, Francis remarked, 'You may as well let me walk without holding on, for I shall not attempt to run away.'

Elizabeth Holloway kept a small stall opposite the *Coach and Horses Inn* and she heard a terrible scream echo from somewhere in Lawrence's Yard. Going to see what had happened, she saw Mary Ann Losch, lying on her back and writhing in terrible pain, her internal organs protruding through a wound in her side. As she looked on in horror, Mrs Holloway saw some men bring candles so that a search could be made for the weapon Francis had used. She saw a man find the bloodstained knife in a gutter and hand it to a constable.

Constable Richard Maybank was on duty in the lock-up when Francis Losch was brought in by Treadway and Carter. After placing Losch in a cell, Constable Maybank went to the scene of the attack, where the knife was handed over to him. A few minutes later, Maybank went to Dr Turnbull's surgery in Sloane

Square. By now, some men had placed Mary Ann on a shutter and carried her to the surgery. When Maybank arrived, the unfortunate woman was still alive, but in acute pain.

John Kitching was the house surgeon at St George's Hospital. He was the first doctor to examine Mary Ann when she was brought in, and he noticed a deep, eight-inch-long wound on the right side of her abdomen. Mary Ann's bowels, and part of her stomach, protruded through the wound. There was very little he could do for her and she died soon after admittance.

The jury at the inquest had little trouble in deciding that Mary Ann had been murdered by her husband. He faced his trial, at the Old Bailey, before Mr Justice Dallas, on 28 October. When all the evidence was heard again, Francis Losch was adjudged to be guilty and sentenced to death.

There was to be no escape from the noose and, on Monday, 2 November, forty-four-year-old Francis Losch was hanged outside Newgate prison. After his body had hung for the statutory hour, it was taken down and sent to St Bartholomew's Hospital for dissection.

Chapter 2

Thomas Birmingham
1829

At approximately 4.10am, on the morning of Thursday, 14 May 1829, William Davis, a watchman, was walking along the bottom of St Mary Abbott's Terrace, Kensington, heading towards the Uxbridge Road, when he noticed a woman lying face down in the road, in Addison's Place.

Rushing to offer what aid he could, William gently turned the lady over and saw that she had received a severe wound in the area of her left breast. Unsure as to whether the poor woman was alive or dead, William ran off to find a surgeon.

The medical gentleman that William Davis found was Dr Henry Parkin and he confirmed that the woman was beyond all aid. His examination showed the one single wound, possibly caused by either a knife, or more probably, a bayonet. The problem now, was to identify her.

In fact, identification of the victim proved to be a rather simple affair, for she did have one most distinguishing feature. The woman found by William Davis had her right eye missing. Publication of this fact led Elizabeth Price to come forward to the police.

Elizabeth explained that she was a prostitute and she had a friend named Mary Ann Waite, who was also a lady of the streets. Mary Ann had lost her right eye and, shown the body of the stabbed woman, Elizabeth confirmed that it was indeed Mary Ann. Elizabeth, however, was able to give the police even more useful information, for she identified a client of the dead woman's, a man who had been with her at least four or five times over the last few weeks. Further, Elizabeth had last seen Mary Ann at around 10.00pm on 13 May, when she had said that she was going to meet up with this gentleman again. His name was Thomas Birmingham and he was a groom to Lieutenant Ives, who was based at Kensington barracks.

Naturally, the next port of call for the police was those barracks, where they spoke to Birmingham. He flatly denied even knowing a girl with only one eye and, since this was clearly a lie, he was taken into custody and charged with murder.

At the inquest, it appeared that the case against Birmingham was certain to collapse. He claimed that he had spent the entire night in his barracks, with a young lady named Susan Bennett, and she confirmed that she had been with Birmingham from around midnight on 13 May, until around 5.00am the following morning. However, under questioning, Miss Bennett broke down and admitted she had lied. She had indeed met Birmingham and gone back to his barracks at midnight but she had seen him leave soon afterwards. She then fell asleep and only woke at 5.00am the next morning as he returned to his room. Birmingham's alibi had collapsed and, despite other factors being contradictory, he was sent to face his trial for murder.

Birmingham's trial opened on 13 June, before Mr Justice Littledale. Mr Curwood and Mr Bodkin acted for the defence whilst the case for the Crown was detailed by Mr Carrington and Mr Adolphus.

Susan Bennett, who had by now been charged with lying at the inquest, elaborated on her story somewhat. She now claimed that a sergeant and a captain at the barracks had told her that she would be rewarded financially, but only if she confirmed Birmingham's story that they had been together all night. Unfortunately, Miss Bennett was unable to identify either of the officers she claimed had tried to bribe her.

Richard Tryvett told the court that he had been on Hammersmith Road at around 2.00am on 14 May, when he had seen a man and a woman arguing. He was certain that the woman was Mary Ann Waite but could not positively identify the man. The man either hit the woman, or pushed her away, whereupon she shouted, 'Do you mean to serve me so?' Some other conversation followed and the couple then walked off together, arm in arm. This testimony showed that, in all probability, Mary Ann was still alive at 2.00am so, if Birmingham could explain where he was at that time, he could not be guilty of murder.

Lieutenant Ferdinand Ives of the 15th Hussars confirmed that the prisoner was his groom. Birmingham was certainly in the barracks at 11.00pm on 13 May, for at that time he helped Ives to dress for a ball he was due to attend.

Sergeant Davidson was also in the barracks on the night in question. He stated that he had risen at 4.55am on 14 May and, just under an hour later, at 5.45am, he saw Birmingham coming down from his room. This suggested that, since otherwise Davidson would have seen him, Birmingham was in his own room by 4.55am at the latest. There was, however, one other witness who did little to help Birmingham's defence.

After his arrest, Birmingham had been held in the New Prison at Clerkenwell. One of his fellow prisoners there was William Lee and he now testified that during the time they were in jail together, Birmingham had confessed his guilt.

That testimony might well have proved to be very damaging for Birmingham but fortunately the defence called two other witnesses, Richard Edwards and Samuel Gower, both officers at the prison, who testified that Lee was a habitual liar.

The jury had a most difficult task. Susan Bennett had first provided an alibi, then admitted she had lied, but could not name the officers she claimed had tried to bribe her. Lieutenant Ives and Sergeant Davidson both claimed that Birmingham was in his barracks all night, even though he had not been seen between around 11.00pm on the 13th and some time after 4.55am on the 14th. In the event, after a very short deliberation, the jury decided that there was not enough evidence to convict and a not guilty verdict was returned.

Twenty-two-year-old Thomas Birmingham was a free man. The murder of Mary Ann Waite remains unsolved to this day.

Chapter 3

The Murder of Catherine Elmes

1833

Catherine Elmes had once run a moderately successful girls' school in Smith Street, Chelsea but, once she had retired from that profession, Catherine had fallen on hard times. By 1833 she was living at 17 Wellesley Street, also in Chelsea, where she eked out a living by taking in the occasional lodger. She was so poor that her rent had to be paid by her brother, 'a reverend gentleman', who usually sent cheques drawn on his solicitor, to cover Catherine's expenses.

Catherine now had few pleasures in life, but one that remained was the occasional half-pint of beer with her supper. It was that which took her to the *Wellesley Arms*, on the evening of Thursday, 2 May 1833, when she took her own pot along and had the half of beer drawn into it. She was then seen, by a few of her neighbours, returning to her home.

No one saw Catherine the next day, Friday. By the day after that, Saturday, 4 May, some of the neighbours were growing a little concerned. One thing that could be said for Catherine, was that she was a creature of habit and people usually saw her pottering about, or going to the local shops, but now she hadn't been seen for two days. Mrs Exley, who lived at number 16, took her concerns to Mr Dorking, a friend of Catherine's, who lived in Blacklands Lane. He returned to Wellesley Street with Mrs Exley and, having knocked a few times and receiving no answer, Mr Dorking decided that it would be best to call in the police.

In due course, Constable Charles Hughes arrived and said that he would force an entry to the premises. Thinking that it might be easier to gain entrance at the back, Hughes obtained a ladder, which he put up to the bedroom on the first floor. Upon gaining access to the bedroom, Constable Hughes saw that it was in a great deal of confusion. Before investigating further, the officer went downstairs so that Mrs Exley, Mr Dorking and another gentleman, Mr Cole, could be admitted. Once they were all inside, Hughes opened the shutters, in order to let some light into the dark rooms. That light revealed the body of Catherine Elmes, lying on the floor, on her stomach, surrounded by a pool of blood.

Catherine had been subjected to a most brutal attack. There was a deep gash over her left eye. So severe was this wound, that the left eyeball had been cut completely in two. A second gash divided the upper part of her nose. The killer had then plunged the knife into Catherine's throat and drawn it violently from side to side. It was also possible that before this, Catherine had been struck with some blunt object, since two of her teeth had been knocked out and lay close by, on a rug.

The motive for this crime appeared to be one of robbery, for clothes were strewn about the floor of the various rooms, cupboards and drawers had been thrown open and their contents scattered about. The problem was, how had the killer gained access? Both the front and back doors had been locked, and all the shutters had been closed and fastened from inside. Either the killer was known to Catherine and had been admitted by her, or he had had a key.

It was this that led the police to their first suspect. At the time she had been attacked, Catherine had had a family lodging with her, a Mrs Mary Ann Eastman and her three children. She rented rooms on the second floor, but had been staying with her sister, who was ill, over the past few days. Even as Constable Hughes and the others carefully looked through the house, Mrs Eastman appeared outside and demanded to be admitted, so that she could check if any of her property had been taken. Questioned by Hughes, she seemed to be very evasive and unwilling to answer so, for that reason, she was arrested and taken to the police station for interview. She was soon able to give a full account of her movements and, once it became clear that she had nothing to do with the crime, Mrs Eastman was released.

The inquest on the dead woman opened on Monday, 6 May, at the *Wellesley Arms*, before the coroner, Mr Stirling. The first step was to take the jury to number 17, where they viewed the body, which had not yet been moved. They then returned to the public house, where the first witness was Constable Hughes. He confirmed that he had been called to Wellesley Street between 3.00pm and 4.00pm and then described what he had found on gaining entry to the house.

Mr Gaskell was the surgeon who had been called to examine the dead woman. He merely reported the details of the terrible wounds that Catherine had suffered. Gaskell was followed to the stand by Sarah Scarlet, the wife of the landlord of the *Wellesley Arms*, who confirmed that Catherine had called for her beer at 10.00pm on 2 May.

James Hunt was the pot-boy at the public house and he testified that he had seen two strange men loitering in the street, at around 8.30pm on 2 May. Hunt was in and out of the bar at various times that night and each time he saw the same men. However, Constable David Costello, who was on duty in and around Wellesley Street on the night in question, said he had walked down the street between 8.00pm and 9.00pm and had seen no men.

This testimony was negated by Constable William Lines, who had taken over Costello's beat at 9.00pm. He said he had seen two strange men on the corner of the street, at around 10.00pm. Constable Lines had asked them what they were doing and they said that they were waiting for a friend.

Mary Ann Eastman said that she had last stayed at Catherine's house on Wednesday, 1 May. Since then she and the children had stayed with her sister, who lived in Manor Street, because one of her children was ill, and she was helping out. The proceedings were then adjourned, pending further police enquiries.

In fact, there was a more specific reason for adjourning the inquest at that stage. The reports of the 'strange men', seen in

Wellesley Street on the night of the murder, led police to concentrate on tracing them. This was actually done quite quickly and so the inquest re-opened on Friday, 10 May, but this time at the workhouse, rather than the local public house.

At the beginning of the proceedings, it was announced that a letter had been received, from the Home Office, confirming that a reward of £100 had been offered for information leading to the arrest of the miscreants in this case. This was followed by Constable Hughes taking the stand again and confirming that in his search of the premises, he had found a short sword and a knotted holly stick, but neither appeared to have been used in the attack upon Catherine Elmes. However, the officer was also able to say that he had found the pot, which Catherine had used to hold the half-pint of beer that she had purchased on the night she had been killed. The pot had been drained of its contents, leading to the conclusion that she must have finished her supper before she was attacked.

The three men seen in the street had, by now, been identified as Roberts, Wheeler and Rickards, and all were called to show that they had perfectly innocent explanations for being in the street on the night of the murder. However, a more promising lead had by now emerged.

Ann Busby was an old friend of the dead woman and she had told the police that at one stage, a few years back, Catherine had had a lodger living with her, who was either a nephew or a cousin of hers. He had taken to using rather foul language and eventually, Catherine had asked him to leave. They did not part on the best of terms and at one stage he had said that he would have his revenge upon her.

In fact, the police had discovered that this man still lived in the area. The man who had been brought into court and another witness, Henry Elmes, who lived at Lancing in Sussex, were able to give some details of Catherine's past. Henry confirmed that Catherine was his sister, and the man now produced in court was her first cousin, a man named William Dagnall.

Dagnall was then called to the stand. He confirmed that he was Catherine's cousin and had lived with her, for a short time, some years before. He denied that she had thrown him out, or that there was any animosity between them. He also claimed that on the night of the murder, he had been at home in bed. The next witness, Anne Quinlin, was Dagnall's step-daughter and lived with him at 13 South Street, Chelsea. She confirmed that he had indeed been at home all that night.

The police had no other leads to go on, and no other suspects, so the jury returned the only possible verdict of murder by person or persons unknown. As the inquest closed, the coroner remarked that investigations were ongoing and that every effort would be made to find the man or men responsible for this terrible deed. In fact, the police did not have to wait for very long before a man came forward and gave himself up for the crime.

On Wednesday, 15 May, a man named John Sharpe, called at the house of Constable Clifton and asked to speak to him. Clifton was not at home at the time and Sharpe was advised to go to the station house in New Way, Tothill Street, which he duly did. There, he identified himself, confirmed that he lodged at 15 Dean Street, Broadway, Westminster and, when asked what he wanted, announced, 'I am one of the men who committed the murder at Chelsea.'

Sharpe had obviously been in a recent fight, for he bore a black eye and a badly scratched face. He went on to explain that he and two other men had broken into the house in Wellesley Street, with the intention of robbery and one of his companions had struck the old woman and then killed her. Over the last couple of days they had argued over another robbery and this argument had ended in a fight. As a result, Sharpe had now decided to give himself up and added that at a later date, possibly before the magistrates, he would name his two companions.

Interviewed at the police station, Sharpe claimed that he and his companions had arrived at Catherine's house at about 8.00pm on the night she was killed and had then hidden for three hours, in the kitchen. After Catherine had been killed they ransacked the house but were disturbed by what they thought was a knock at the front door. Going out the back way they then went around into Wellesley Street and discovered that the 'knock' was nothing more than a drunken man falling against the door.

John Sharpe appeared before the magistrates the next day, 16 May, where details of his arrest and statement were given. It was also revealed that he had previously come to the attention of the authorities, for passing base coinage. He was then remanded in custody.

Even at this early stage, doubts were expressed as to whether John Sharpe was actually telling the truth. A newspaper report of 20 May confirmed that Sharpe was a most unsavoury character. He was a married man but had left his wife some years ago, to live with another woman. Their relationship was a most violent one and the police had been called to his house many times, to restore the peace. Twelve months ago, Sharpe had walked into a police station, with a pile of bloody clothing, and confessed that he had murdered his two children. He was arrested at that time, but subsequent investigations revealed that the children had both died of the measles some months before. As for the blood on the clothing, that belonged to Sharpe himself and had been deposited there after yet another violent argument with his lover.

By 30 May, when Sharpe made his next appearance in court, he had completely withdrawn his confession and claimed that he knew nothing whatsoever of the murder. After yet another argument, he had assaulted his common-law wife and she had taken out the summons and the only reason he had given himself up in the first place, was to avoid that being served upon him.

There were, however, two problems for Sharpe to overcome. The first of these was that he had given a fairly accurate report of what must have actually happened inside the murder house. That was, possibly, explained by Sharpe's claim that he had read those details in the local newspapers, but the second factor was more difficult to explain.

In his statement, Sharpe had referred to he and his companions leaving the house when a drunken man fell against the door. One of Catherine Elmes' neighbours, Mrs Elizabeth

Ington, had reported to the police that she had actually seen a drunk fall against the door at almost exactly the time Sharpe had stated. For that reason, although there was no other reason to hold him, Sharpe was remanded in custody yet again.

Sharpe made his final court appearance, in respect of the murder of Catherine Elmes, on 5 June. By that date the authorities had come to accept that he had had no involvement in the crime and was discharged. However, there remained the matter of his assault upon his lover, Hannah Heywood, and it was decided that, since she was in fear of a further assault, Sharpe must supply two sureties of £20 each. Sharpe said that he could not afford such a sum and begged Hannah to pay it for him. She refused, so Sharpe was committed to the next Middlesex sessions.

In the event, Sharpe did manage to obtain the sureties he required and he was discharged from prison towards the end of June. He immediately returned to his lodgings to collect some of his belongings, which Hannah Heywood refused to give him. When he complained to the police, they advised him to seek the aid of a solicitor and the matter was then dropped. As for the killer of Catherine Elmes, he was never traced and the murder remains unsolved.

Chapter 4

William Jarman
1837

The relationship between William Jarman and his wife, Esther, was not all it should be and there were constant arguments between them, especially when William had been drinking. After one such argument, in early December 1837, William struck out at Esther and she swore that she would issue a summons against him, for assault. However, before any action could be taken on Esther's complaint, a new development would occur.

On the evening of Wednesday, 13 December 1837, Dr William Hayward Robinson was called to Jarman's house in Kensington where he found William sitting in a chair, suffering from delirium tremens after his latest drinking bout. William also had a severe contusion on his left arm, which might have been caused by some sort of sharp instrument. For the time being at least, Dr Robinson decided that no further treatment was necessary, but he did promise to call again the next day.

Dr Robinson did indeed call again on the morning of Thursday, 14 December, and found William Jarman still suffering from the effects of drink. During the examination, William asked the doctor to take a look at his wife, who was sitting in a chair near the fire. Dr Robinson did as he was asked and found that Esther's pulse was weak and quick. Concerned that she might be suffering from some kind of fever, Dr Robinson decided that it would be best to bleed his patient from the arm. He then duly took thirteen ounces of blood, bandaged the wound and ordered Esther to bed.

Later that same day, Dr Robinson decided to call on Esther again. He found Esther's married daughter, Esther Lidford, waiting to speak to him. Mrs Lidford pointed out to Dr

Robinson that since his last visit, the wound in her mother's arm seemed to have opened up again, as she had started to bleed rather freely. Dr Robinson went to the bedroom to check on Esther and found that he was too late. She had passed away and the bed was extensively stained with blood.

Since this entire affair had come about through the possible ill-treatment of Esther by her husband, the police were called in and William Jarman was duly arrested and charged with murder. He appeared before the magistrates on Friday, 15 December.

One of the first witnesses was Police Sergeant Tringham who testified that he had first heard of Esther's death late on the evening of 14 December. He had then gone to Jarman's house, with Sergeant Clarke, where they had viewed the dead body of Esther Jarman. There were extensive bruises on her body and a good deal of blood about the bed, especially on the pillows.

Rebecca Lloyd had been a friend of the dead woman and had called at her house, by invitation, on Wednesday, 13 December. After testifying that she had seen Jarman strike his wife on a number of occasions, she told the court that when she had left their home on Wednesday night, Jarman had simply closed the door on her without as much as a goodbye.

After those few witnesses had given their evidence, Mr Pilkington, the magistrate, decided to adjourn matters until after the inquest, when the subject of Esther's death could be gone into more closely. Jarman, however, was remanded in custody.

The inquest opened on Monday, 18 December, before Mr Stirling, the coroner, at the *Wellington Arms Tavern* in South Street, Kensington. The first witness was Dr Robinson, who detailed his treatment of Esther Jarman. He explained that he had called, for the final time, on the Thursday evening. He was examining William Jarman when Esther's daughter came downstairs and said her mother had started bleeding badly from the wound in her arm. He had gone upstairs and applied pressure to the wound, with his thumb. Perhaps the most telling part of Dr Robinson's testimony, was that he initially believed that Esther had merely fainted when, in fact, she was quite dead. Under intense cross-examination, Dr Robinson had to agree that the direct cause of death had been due to loss of blood.

A somewhat feeble attempt was made to place the blame for Esther's death on her husband's shoulders. His daughter, Mrs Lidford, testified that her father was a most violent man, especially in drink, but she could refer to no recent incident where she had actually witnessed such violence.

Sarah Sheen, a neighbour, said she had seen Jarman attack his wife, with his fists, several times in the past but, under cross-examination, she also had to admit that Esther was also a most irritable woman and often gave as good as she got.

There was, of course, no real evidence against William. He may have been violent towards his wife, but it was clear that her death had been caused by the wound inflicted in her arm by Dr Robinson, and also, perhaps, by his lack of care afterwards. The jury returned the verdict that Esther had 'died from the loss of blood occasioned by the opening of the vein'. In short, William Jarman was not responsible for his wife's death and he had no charge to answer. Neither, it appeared, had Dr Robinson, for no charge was ever laid against him.

Chapter 5

William John Marchant
1839

The Edgell family lived in some degree of luxury at their house at 21 Cadogan Place. They had a number of servants including a housekeeper, a coachman, an upper footman, a cook, an upper housemaid, an under housemaid and a footman. Their life was very comfortable indeed.

On Friday, 17 May 1839, the Edgells wished to travel to Crayford in Kent, to visit some friends. Taking most of their staff with them on the journey, they only left four servants in the house: the cook, the housemaid, Elizabeth Paynter, the under housemaid and William John Marchant, the footman. The entire entourage left Cadogan Place at approximately 2.00pm.

Once they had finished their allotted work, at 3.30pm, the cook and the housemaid left to visit some friends of their own, leaving just Elizabeth Paynter, who preferred to be called Ann, and Marchant alone in the house.

At 6.00pm, the cook returned but found the front door of the house locked. She rang the bell and knocked stridently at the door, but there was no reply. In fact, she continued trying to gain entrance until almost 7.00pm, but there was still no sign of anyone in the house. The cook was eventually joined by the housemaid, Elizabeth Gough, and the two ladies tried their best to rouse someone inside the house, but it was all to no avail.

Some time later, the coachman returned, having dropped the Edgells off in Kent. He was with the upper footman and, having listened to the story from the cook and Elizabeth Gough, they decided that it would be best to force an entry at the back of the house. The door was duly smashed open and the four staff members went inside to search the premises, in an attempt to find out why no one had bothered to let them in.

Elizabeth Gough decided that she would search the rooms on the ground floor and it was when she walked into the drawing room that the reason for their non-admittance was revealed. There lay the body of Elizabeth Paynter, on the floor. Her throat had been cut and she was quite plainly beyond all human aid. Of William John Marchant, the other servant, there was no sign whatsoever.

The upper footman, taking charge of the situation, ran to the surgery of Dr Henry Jay at 42 Sloane Street. He attended immediately and confirmed that Elizabeth was dead. In his estimation, she had been dead for between three and four hours. Dr Jay also made a quick search of the room and discovered a bloodstained razor some feet from the body.

A massive police search was launched for the missing man, Marchant, but at 6.00pm on Saturday 18 May, he surrendered himself to a police officer near Ascot, admitting that he had killed a young woman in London. He later made a full statement, after which he was duly charged with murder.

The inquest on Elizabeth Paynter opened on Monday, 20 May, before the coroner, Mr Wakley. After evidence of the finding of the body had been detailed, Inspector William Lawrence was called to the stand. He testified that Marchant had approached him and explained that he wished to surrender himself to the police. Inspector Lawrence had asked him what for and Marchant had replied, 'For the murder of a young woman at number twenty one Cadogan Place in London.'

Taken to the police station, Marchant had been interviewed and he went on to detail his movements after he had cut Elizabeth's throat. He had travelled to Windsor and spent some time at the *Two Brewers* public house, before walking on towards Ascot. Along the way he decided that he would give himself up to the first police officer he saw.

Another police witness was Sergeant Morris Mulcahy, who had attended the scene at Cadogan Place. He had made a careful examination of the entire house and, in the pantry downstairs, had found a bloodstained towel. The inference was that Marchant had committed the crime upstairs in the drawing room, taken the towel to wipe the blood from his hands and dropped this in the pantry, as he made good his escape through the back door.

Sergeant Mulcahy was also able to state that there were obvious signs of a struggle in the drawing room and Elizabeth had fought for her life. She had some hair clutched in her right hand and this matched Marchant's hair. When her body was discovered, her stockings were drawn half way down her legs and the suggestion was that Marchant had tried to force himself upon her. She had resisted and he had killed her.

The various members of staff from the house at Cadogan Place were all called to give their evidence. They all said that Marchant was a most diligent worker and the household had never had any trouble with him. He was, at nineteen, still a very young man, but this was his second position in service. Previously he had been a page at the home of Mr Elwyn at 84 Cadogan Place and he had come to number 21 with an excellent reference. As for his relationship with the dead woman, he had always behaved properly towards her and there was no suggestion of any physical relationship between them.

The inquest duly returned a verdict of murder against Marchant and he was sent for trial. That trial took place at the Old Bailey on 23 June, when Marchant pleaded guilty to the charge. There could only be one result of the plea and Marchant was then sentenced to death.

William Marchant did not escape the noose and, on 8 July 1839, was hanged outside Newgate prison. It was the seventh execution of the year, but the first one in London.

Chapter 6

Robert Williamson
1842

There were a number of people lodging at 12 Royal Hospital Row, in Chelsea. One couple, Margaret and John Doolen, occupied rooms on the ground floor and on the evening of Wednesday, 26 October 1842, at around 5.00pm, both were enjoying their meal together when, suddenly, a blood-curdling scream rang out.

The scream had come from the direction of the stairs and Margaret Doolen immediately dashed out to investigate. She found Sarah Williamson, the woman who lived upstairs, using one hand to support herself against the banister. Her other hand she held underneath her chin and there appeared to be blood everywhere. Sarah explained that her husband, Robert, had just attacked her with a poker and struck her 'about the top of her head'.

Margaret helped Sarah into her own rooms and sat her down on a chair. It was clear that the wound would need proper medical attention so Margaret took her wounded neighbour to see a doctor in George Street. He dressed the wound and Margaret then escorted Sarah to her daughter's house.

Esther Tanner was Sarah's daughter by her first husband and she insisted that her mother should be taken to the hospital. A cab was called and Esther took Sarah to St George's Hospital, where she was seen by the house surgeon, Dr George Augustus Davis. He timed her arrival at a few minutes before 7.00pm and he noted a single deep wound on the crown of Sarah's head. The skin was broken and Dr Davis could see the bone beneath but there did not appear to be any fracture of the skull. He also noted a second wound, on Sarah's left arm and decided that both may well have been caused by a poker, used with some considerable degree of violence.

The police were called and Sarah Williamson was able to make a full statement to them. In this she explained that she and Robert had been together in the *Coach and Horses* public house for two or three hours and had left together at some time between 4.00pm and 5.00pm. Once they were inside their lodgings, Robert had called her an old whore, picked up a poker and said that he was going to murder her. Even before she could reply to this threat, Sarah received a massive blow on her head. She was dazed but managed to stagger out of the room and down the stairs. Robert, however, followed her and struck her a second time, catching her on the arm. It was at that point that Margaret Doolen had come to her aid.

Initially, Sarah Williamson responded to the medical treatment she received. For a time her condition improved but then, on 14 November, she fell ill again. This time she grew steadily worse and, on Saturday, 19 November, she died. Robert, who had previously been charged with assaulting his wife, now found himself facing a charge of murder, in addition to the one of assault.

Robert Williamson faced his trial on 28 November 1842. In addition to the evidence of Margaret Doolen, the court heard from her husband, John. He testified that he had also heard the scream, but left it to his wife to attend to the stricken woman. After Margaret and Sarah had left to go to the doctor's, John heard a great deal of noise from the rooms upstairs. It sounded like breaking crockery and at one stage he heard Robert shout, 'I will let them see who is master in this house.'

After his arrest, Robert had made an appearance before the magistrates at the Queen Street police court. After the proceedings had concluded he made a statement to the chief clerk, Richard Edwards, and this was taken down in writing. That statement was now read out to the court.

Robert began by saying, 'I can only say she had been out and got drunk, and I left her at the *Coach and Horses* public house. I went home and lit the fire and boiled the kettle. She then came home. I went to make the tea and found tea-leaves in the pot and I asked her if she had had any tea.'

'She said, "Damn you and your tea too." I had put hot water to the tea-leaves in the pot and she took up the pot and threw it, and the water, at me. The hot water came all over my face. She then set to and broke the tea things and plates. She then went out to go downstairs and she stumbled down two pairs of stairs.'

This statement did not seem to agree with what Esther Tanner, Sarah's daughter, had to say. After seeing her mother to the hospital, she had gone to visit her stepfather at Royal Hospital Row. She told him that his wife was in hospital and very badly injured. He replied, 'A good job and a very good job if she went mad, for I do not want to have anything more to do with the gang of you.'

It seemed clear that this had been a domestic argument, which had got out of hand. It fell to the jury to decide if that argument had been instigated by Robert, or by his wife. In the event, they decided that Robert was not guilty of murder, but was guilty of assaulting his wife. Further, they recommended him to mercy on account of the provocation he had received and his previous good character. The judge took that into consideration and sentenced Robert to just one year in prison.

Chapter 7

Michael and Ann Connell
1851

George Ferris had had enough. It was 1.00am on the morning of Sunday, 6 April 1851, and his lodgers, who lived downstairs, at 2 Exeter Place, Chelsea, were keeping him awake by arguing yet again.

In fact, there were four lodgers living together downstairs. In addition to Michael Connell and his wife, Ann, there was also Caroline Jewel, a friend of theirs who shared their rooms. The fourth lodger was the Connell's small son, six-year-old Daniel. Unfortunately, it seemed that all of the three adults had something of a drink problem and, once they were under the influence, there was always something new to argue about.

When George went downstairs to sort this matter out, he found Ann and Michael squaring up to each other and Caroline sitting on a chair nearby. As George warned them that if they didn't keep the noise down he would go for a constable, a 'strange woman' walked in from the next room.

Even before George could ask who this woman was, Ann moved forward and struck Michael in the face. In response, Michael grabbed his wife by the hair and struck her two or three times. George again asked them to settle down and now demanded to know who this other woman was.

Ann replied that she had just come home and found Michael with this woman. In an attempt to cool the situation down, George told the strange woman that it would probably be better if she were to leave. The woman, thinking that this was good advice, opened the door and left, only to be followed by Ann who struck out at her on the landing outside. Finally, the woman managed to make good her escape and a rather weary George Ferris made his way back to his welcoming bed.

George was not, however, to gain much respite for, some ten minutes later, there was a knock on his door. Opening it with a deep sigh, George found Michael Connell, who asked him to come back to their rooms, as he believed someone was dead. Taking a candle for extra light, George returned to the Connell's rooms to find Caroline Jewel lying on her back, with a red mark across her nose, as if she had received a blow of some kind. There was no sign of Ann Connell.

It was time to bring in the authorities and the first officer on the scene was Sergeant George Tewsley. Having sent for the doctor, who pronounced Caroline to be dead, Tewsley then took the only other occupant of the room, Michael Connell, into custody on a charge of manslaughter.

At the police station, Michael was interviewed by Inspector Robert McKenzie, to whom he made a full statement. It began, 'I did not cause her death at all. Me and my old woman were having a fight and she stood up between us. Whether I struck her or not, I cannot say. My old woman came home and, seeing a strange woman there, commenced a row.'

Later in that same statement, Michael said that after the argument he suddenly noticed Caroline Jewel on the floor, thought she was just stunned, and asked her to get up. He then made some tea and tried to lift Caroline up. At the time, her legs were moving and she groaned a little but when he could not rouse her, he went to Mr Ferris for help.

A few hours after this, Ann Connell was also arrested and charged with the same offence as her husband. Later, however, at the inquest on the dead woman, the charge against both of the Connell's was amended to one of 'causing the death of Caroline Jewel'.

The trial of both defendants took place on 12 May 1851. After George Ferris and the police had given their evidence, the prosecution called young Daniel Connell whose simple testimony was, 'Mother pushed Mrs Jewel down and she went dead.'

The post-mortem on Caroline had been carried out by Mr Frederick Sotherby Miller, who found a large blood clot in her head. Several blood vessels had ruptured and broken and the brain was floating on a large quantity of blood.

By now, the strange woman at the scene had been traced and she now gave the court her testimony. Susannah Blanchfield said that on Saturday, 5 April, she had left the service of Mr Sturry, at 7 Denbigh Place, Pimlico. She had intended staying that night at a friend's house, at 1 Ann Place, Knightsbridge but, on arrival there, Susannah found that her friend was not at home. She left her trunks there, in the care of a servant, and then went to sit in the nearby park.

Susannah had only been in the park a short time when Ann Connell approached her. The two women fell into conversation and, concerned that it was now growing rather late, Susannah asked Ann if she knew of a place where she might sleep for just that one night. Ann invited her back to 2 Exeter Place, where Susannah had tea with Ann, Michael and Caroline.

In due course, Susannah went to bed, but she was soon roused from her slumber by someone fondling her body. She woke to find that Michael Connell was molesting her and when she remonstrated with him, he said that if she cried out or resisted him, he would smash her head in. He then stole her purse from her.

Very soon after this, Ann returned home and upon seeing Susannah, and apparently forgetting that she had invited her home in the first place, flew at her and struck out at her. Finally, just before Susannah managed to escape from the house, she saw Ann seize Caroline Jewel and throw her to the floor. She noticed that, as she landed, Caroline struck her head hard at the back.

After hearing all the evidence, the jury decided that Michael Connell was in no way responsible for Caroline's death, and he was acquitted. Ann, however, was judged to be guilty and was given the perhaps somewhat light sentence of two months' imprisonment, with the last week to be served in solitary confinement.

Chapter 8

James Mooney
1867

Ann Mooney had been married to her husband for some six years and they had one son, John, who was now five years old. The marital relationship, however, was a tempestuous one, James regularly assaulting his wife.

During the evening of Saturday, 29 December 1866, Ann was having a quiet, and totally innocuous conversation with a young man, who had been a friend of the family for a number of years. Suddenly, her husband strode up behind her, struck her on her back and demanded that she should return immediately to their home, at 9 Pembroke Place, Earl Street, Kensington. Anxious to avoid a scene in the street, Ann did as he had demanded.

Once inside the house, James's temper did not improve. He immediately stripped his wife naked, hit her on the side of her face and threw most of her clothing onto the fire. Even now James had not finished with Ann. He beat her again and, by the time he had finished with her, she was barely able to stand. So bad did the assault become, that even their child shouted, 'Mother, hide under the bed, father will kill you.'

As James ended his attack upon his wife, she managed to pull on a single, flimsy undergarment and run out into the yard at the back of the house. There she was seen by a neighbour, Hannah Penton, who took Ann inside and gave her some of her own clothes. Ann decided that it would be best if she stayed with Hannah, at least for the time being.

The next day, Sunday, 30 December, Ann Hayes, who lived at 8 Pembroke Place, decided to call on Ann Mooney during the morning. She did not know that Ann was staying, temporarily, with Hannah Penton, so obviously did not find Ann at home. Five-year-old John Mooney was at home, however, and Ann

Hayes found him lying in his bed, apparently in some distress. Ann asked the boy where his parents were and John replied, 'Poor mother ran away, and naughty father burnt me.'

At first, Ann did not really grasp the severity of what John had just said. Eventually she realised that this might well be a most serious matter and took her information to the police. That in turn led to a visit from Inspector Cross who visited the Mooney's home later that same Sunday. He found that the bed quilt covering John showed signs of burning. Of John himself there was now no sign, but later Cross discovered that James Mooney had taken him to the hospital for treatment. That effort had proved to be rather too late and John Mooney had since died. Later, Inspector Cross traced James Mooney and arrested him on a charge of assaulting his wife, Ann, and of killing his child, by burning him.

James Mooney appeared before the magistrates on Monday, 31 December. After Ann Mooney, Hannah Penton and Ann Hayes had given their testimony, Inspector Cross stepped forward to detail his evidence.

Cross stated that when he had visited the house at Pembroke Place, he had seen ashes in the fire-grate which were consistent with the burning of some clothing. He had then examined the quilt on John Mooney's bed and found that it was burnt at one end. Turning the quilt over, he found three small circular burn holes and evidence that water had been thrown over the bed.

Once James Mooney had been arrested and taken to the police station, he made a full statement giving his version of what had happened to his son. James said that he had left his son alone in the house when he went out to look for his wife. At the time, there was a single candle burning in the room, close to his son's bed. When James returned home, the bedroom was in darkness so he asked John what had happened to the candle. John replied that it was in bed and when James lit a match, he saw that his son's quilt was smouldering. It was James who ran for some water and threw it over his son's bed. The next morning, John had complained that he had been burned and James then took him to the hospital.

Dr FH Sims was the house surgeon at St George's Hospital. He confirmed that John had been brought in by his father on the Sunday morning. The child was quite badly burned on the back part of his thighs, his groin and also around his heels. He died within a few hours.

Matters were then adjourned to 4 January and on that date, no further evidence was offered against James Mooney, chiefly because, in the meantime, the inquest on John had returned a verdict of accidental death. There remain, however, a number of unanswered questions.

John Mooney had originally told Ann Hayes that it had been his father who had burned him. James, then said that the fire had been accidental, when either the candle had fallen into the bed or, more likely perhaps, John had been playing with it when his quilt caught fire.

If the first of those scenarios was the truth then James Mooney should have faced a charge of either murder or manslaughter. If, however, the second is true, and this was a tragic accident, why did the child not complain of the pain on the night that it happened? It is possible, though, that having seen what had happened to his mother, John had been afraid to tell his father the extent of the damage done to the quilt, so could not mention the damage to himself. It is still, at the very least, most unusual behaviour for a five-year-old.

It may well be that John Mooney was killed by his father, who then escaped the consequences of his cruel action.

Chapter 9

Walter Miller
1870

I t was the usual sort of job for Mr Henry Piper. A gentleman had asked him to remove some furniture and packing cases from a house and take them to another address in Fulham Road and, at least to begin with, everything had gone well.

A number of items had been loaded onto the cart outside 15 Paulton's Square, King's Road, Chelsea, on this evening of Wednesday, 11 May 1870, and the time came to load a large box. Piper noticed that the cord tied around the box had not been fastened very securely and said that he would fix it before he tried to lift the box. To his surprise, the man who had employed him suddenly dashed forward and said that he would re-tie the cord himself. Gently, Piper told the man that he was much more used to such things and would do a proper job of it. Rather reluctantly, the man allowed Piper to begin but, even as he pulled the heavy box forward, Piper noticed a crimson liquid issuing from one corner.

Piper demanded to know what was inside the box and was told that it was nothing of consequence and asked to get on with tying it up. Piper refused and said that he would do no more work until he knew what was going on.

For a few moments there was nothing but silence. The young man who had employed him just stared at him, as did the two women who were also present. Then, suddenly, the man and the younger of the two women ran off; she upstairs and he out into the street. Piper was having none of this and followed the man outside. Fortunately there was a police constable nearby and Piper called out for him to seize the man. He was duly taken and escorted back to the house.

The officer, Constable Joseph Giles, told Piper that he would need some assistance if he was to keep hold of his man and examine the heavy box in the house. Piper said that he would go off and find another constable and walked away. He had not gone more than a few yards when a shout revealed that the prisoner had made a dash for it. Both Piper and Constable Giles gave chase and it was Piper who was closest when the man stumbled and fell in Church Street. Once again he was marched back to the house in Paulton's Square and, soon afterwards, another officer arrived. An inspection of the packing case was made and this revealed the body of a young woman, doubled over inside the box. Blood had issued from the woman's nose and mouth and she was undoubtedly dead. It appeared to be a clear case of murder and the young man who had employed Piper, Walter Miller, was taken into custody.

Police enquiries soon revealed that the house at 15 Paulton's Square belonged to a retired clergyman named Elias Huelin and he lived there with his housekeeper, Anne Boss. Further enquiries showed that dead woman in the packing case was Anne Boss but, of her employer, Mr Huelin, there was no sign.

A number of neighbours were spoken to and, from these interviews, it became clear that Mr Huelin and his housekeeper had not been seen since Monday, 9 May. It was on that day, at 7.00am, that John Hunt had seen Miss Boss cleaning the front steps of the house. Mr Hunt, and other neighbours, knew that Mr Huelin had a farm in Lincolnshire and he had been discussing going there for a short holiday. They had all simply believed that he had left and had therefore seen nothing suspicious in him not being seen for some days.

The inquest on Ann Boss opened at the *Black Lion Inn* on Thursday, 12 May. Here, Henry Piper explained that Miller had come to his house in Marlborough Road, the previous night. He had mentioned the moving of some furniture and boxes and Piper had said that he would call the following day. Miller replied that it was an urgent job and he must come right away. Rather reluctantly, Piper had agreed and arrived at the house at 9.00pm, the front door being opened by an elderly lady. The box containing the body was in the kitchen and Piper stated that after he had seen the blood issuing from the corners he had stood up and said, 'Oh I must know what this is before I take it away.' It was soon after this that Miller and a young woman had run off.

The inquest was soon adjourned, pending further inquiries into the whereabouts of Mr Huelin. Reports of the proceedings appeared in the newspapers of Friday, 13 May and this brought Edward James Payne to call in at the police station that same day.

Payne explained that he had known Miller for some three years and, on Monday, 9 May, the last day Mr Huelin and his housekeeper had been seen alive, Miller had approached him outside the *Admiral Keppel Inn* on Brompton Road and asked him if he would do some work for him. Apparently, Miller wanted to replace some drains at a house in Wellington Square and wanted a large ditch dug in the yard.

Payne agreed to do the work and went home to get his pick and shovel. Returning to the *Admiral Keppel*, the two men had a pint together before going off to 24 Wellington Square. Miller had a key to the house and both men went through, into the yard. Miller then watched as Payne dug a hole some three feet deep and seven feet long. By the time it grew dark, the work was still unfinished and Payne said he would return the next day. Payne did return on the Tuesday and Wednesday, but got no reply.

The police knew that 24 Wellington Square was another house that belonged to Mr Huelin. Taking Payne with them, a number of officers went to that address and Payne pointed out where the ditch, by now filled in, had been. The police began to dig and, in due course, Detective Edward Cluff and Detective William Watts, found the body of Mr Huelin. There was a rope tied tightly around his neck but the cause of death had been two deep puncture wounds behind his right ear. Walter Miller was now facing two charges of murder.

In British courts, no matter how many victims a killer may claim, it is customary to hear evidence on just one of the charges. Thus, when Walter Miller faced his trial, before the Lord Chief Justice, on 11 July, the prosecution only proceeded on the murder of Elias Huelin. That prosecution was detailed by Mr Poland and Mr Beasley, whilst Miller was defended by Mr Collins and Mr St Aubyn.

The early witnesses all gave testimony that put Miller in Wellington Square, where the body was later found, on Monday, 9 May. Thus, Robert Cox, who had known Miller for many years, said that he had seen him in the square at 11.00am. A later sighting was made by Thomas Humble Walker, who lived at number 6. He had actually seen Miller going up the steps of number 24 and letting himself in with a key, at around 11.15am.

Other witnesses were able to show that, in all probability, Mr Heulin and Miss Boss were dead before noon on 9 May. Sidney Ball was a baker and he delivered regularly to the house in Paulton's Square. He had called at the house at sometime between noon and 1.00pm on Monday, 9 May, but received no reply to his ringing the bell.

Samuel Stainsby lived next door to Mr Huelin's house, at 14 Paulton's Square. On the evening of 9 May, he had noticed Mr Huelin's dog whining on the front doorstep. Going to investigate, Stainsby had looked over the wall at the back of the house and saw that the windows were open. Thinking that this was unusual, he had gone to find a policeman and two constables had gone back to the house with him. The three men climbed over the yard wall and found that the back door was closed but unlocked. Going inside the house they found that there was apparently no one at home but there was also no sign of any break-in or of any other disorder. The three men left the house at around 11.15pm.

Mr Stainsby was, however, able to give even more information. At about 10.30pm the next day, Tuesday, 10 May, he had seen a cab pull up outside number 15. Miller had alighted and gone up to the door of Mr Huelin's house where he had been let in by an elderly woman. There was some conversation and the cab driver went inside, briefly, before coming out again. It was then that Stainsby heard the cabbie shout, 'Nine o'clock tomorrow then.'

Fortunately for the police, Stainsby had the foresight to take the plate number of the cab.

That number, 4746, led the police to Thomas Herbert, who confirmed that Miller had hailed him at Cremorne Gardens on 10 May. Herbert thought that Miller must be foreign as he spoke in broken English with what appeared to be a French accent. Herbert was told to drive to 15 Paulton's Square, but along the journey, his passenger changed his mind and ordered him to 9 Park Walk. After Miller had had some discussion with a few of the householders in that thoroughfare, he had told Herbert to go on to his original destination at Paulton's Square, where he invited him in for a glass of wine. Herbert was more concerned for his fare and declined the offer but, going inside to collect his money, was told that Miller did not have enough cash on him at the time. He was told to return at 9.00pm the next night, when he would receive ten shillings for his trouble. That was the meaning of the parting comment he had made, and which had been overheard by Mr Stainsby.

At the time of Miller's arrest, there had been two women inside the house at Paulton's Square. The first of these was Harriett Middleton who lived at 2 Sidney Mews, Fulham Road. She and Miller had once lodged at the same address so she knew him quite well. She also knew Mr Huelin and had done some work for him quite recently.

On 7 May, some painting work had been finished at 24 Wellington Square. Indeed, Miller had been one of the painters working at that address and, once he and the others had finished, Mrs Middleton was asked to clean the place up a little. This she did and that evening, went to 15 Paulton's Square to collect her money. She was paid by Anne Boss.

On the night of Monday, 9 May, Harriett Middleton was roused from her bed by a strident knocking at her front door. Going downstairs she saw a man she did not recognise at the time, but who she now knew to be Miller, in disguise. He spoke in broken English with a French accent and explained that he was Mr Huelin's nephew, and had just arrived from France. He went on to say that Mr Huelin had gone to his farm in

Lincolnshire and had asked that she take care of the house in Paulton's Square for him. Harriett did as the 'nephew' asked and was there when the cab driver was offered a glass of wine and when Mr Piper moved the box containing the body of Anne Boss.

The younger woman present at that time had been Elizabeth Green. She testified that she had only met Miller on Wednesday, 11 May, in Windmill Street, near the Haymarket. They fell into conversation and he invited her to take a drink with him in a local public house. Miller spent some time with her and treated her very well indeed. Later, he had taken her shopping and purchased a hat, a jacket, a skirt and some boots for her. Later he had taken her to the house in Paulton's Square, where the door was opened by Harriett Middleton. Elizabeth was still in the house when Mr Piper called to move some items to another house.

The prosecution case was that Miller, having done some painting for Mr Huelin, found out that he was a man of wealth and property and decided to steal what he could for himself. Having killed both Huelin and his housekeeper, Miller stole what he could and then set about disposing of the bodies. At one stage he masqueraded as Mr Huelin's French nephew so that, if his crime came to be discovered, the police would be looking for someone other than himself. He might well have gotten away with this plan, but for the prompt action of Henry Piper.

The jury had little problem in returning a guilty verdict and Walter Miller was sentenced to death. As for Henry Piper, the judge awarded him fifty shillings from public funds, as a reward.

Held in Newgate prison, Miller tried to avoid his fate by throwing himself, head first, at a wall. He suffered only cuts and bruises and, as a result, had to be carried to the gallows in a chair on Monday, 1 August 1870. For that reason, the hangman, William Calcraft, gave him an even shorter drop than usual, with the result that Miller strangled slowly at the end of the rope.

Chapter 10

Frances Stewart
1874

Forty-year-old Frances Stewart lived with her married daughter, Henrietta Scrivener, at 4 Lordship Place, Chelsea. There were two other people living in the house, Henrietta's husband, Joseph, and their son, Henry Ernest, who was just over one year old. Unfortunately, neither Henrietta nor Joseph seemed to get on with Frances and there was, therefore, a great deal of tension in the household.

In mid-April 1874, Joseph had a major argument with his mother-in-law. This in turn led to some discussion between Joseph and Henrietta, who agreed that this state of affairs simply could not continue. Having decided on a course of action, both Joseph and his wife spoke to Frances on Monday, 27 April. Joseph told her that either, she must leave the house, or he and his family would. Henrietta told Frances a slightly different story, saying that she, Joseph and Henry were going away as soon as they could find fresh lodgings.

Frances thought about these discussions overnight and the next day, Tuesday, 28 April, she informed both her daughter and son-in-law that she would be '...away before night'. At last, it seemed that an amicable solution had been found to all the family friction.

Frances Stewart was as good as her word and she did walk out of 4 Lordship Place that same day. Unfortunately she took young Henry with her and left behind a note saying that they would both be in the water before long. A frantic Henrietta immediately contacted the police.

The next day, Wednesday, 29 April, Joseph Scrivener received a letter. Written in Frances's hand it read:

I have just left Mrs Sparville. If you or your wife had done what I told you, you would have found your child. It is the only thing I can do to make your heart ache, as you have made mine for so long you bastards, and the dear boy will be no more. We are in the water at this moment.

Joseph knew that the woman referred to in the letter was Charlotte Sparville, an old family friend, who lived at 23 Spencer Road, Fulham. He dashed around to her house and she informed him that Frances had called there at around midnight on the Tuesday. Frances had had the baby with her and asked if she could stay that night, adding that there had been some unpleasantness back at Lordship Place. Permission was granted, Charlotte thinking that this was nothing more than a mild family disagreement, that would soon be sorted out.

At around noon the next day, Charlotte had asked Frances if she was going to return home to Lordship Place and Frances had said that she hadn't made her mind up yet. At that, Charlotte suggested that she should, at the very least, take the boy back to his parents. No more was said and, not long afterwards, Frances and Henry left Charlotte's house.

Joseph Scrivener took this information to the police and they, as part of their ongoing investigation, then warned all known friends and relatives of the missing woman to be on the look-out for her and report it immediately if they saw her. It was this action which led directly to Frances's arrest.

Caroline Stewart was another of Frances's daughters and she worked at *Bacon's Hotel*, which was situated on Great Queen Street. On Friday, 1 May, at some time between 4.00pm and 5.00pm, Frances walked into the foyer of the hotel and asked to speak to her daughter. Caroline was fully aware of the police search for Frances and told the manager to call a constable, whilst she spoke to her mother. The police duly arrived, arrested Frances and allowed Caroline to walk with her mother, to the police station. On the way, Frances mentioned to her daughter that she had left a letter for her, at the hotel. Later, when Caroline collected that letter she read, to her horror, a full confession from Frances, admitting that she had thrown Henry into the Thames at Chelsea.

Henry Ernest Scrivener's body was not found until the following day, Saturday, 2 May. The body was washed up near Millwall and positively identified, by his mother, Henrietta, the following Friday. Frances Stewart, meanwhile, was charged with the wilful murder of her grandson.

Frances Stewart faced her trial on 8 June, before Mr Justice Blackburn. Mr Poland appeared for the prosecution and Mr Straight represented the prisoner.

The first witness was Henrietta Scrivener who told the court of the troubles the family had had and their decision that either Frances must go, or they would. After detailing the search for their son, Henrietta also confirmed that, on Friday 8 May, she had been taken to the mortuary by Inspector Sherlock, where she identified the body of her son.

After Joseph Scrivener and Charlotte Sparville had given their testimony, Ann Ireland took the stand. She said that she lived at 20 Lawrence Street, Chelsea but, on Wednesday, 29 April, she had been in the Fulham Road when she saw Frances, with the baby. It was then 8.15pm and quite a cold night.

The two women fell into conversation and Ann remarked, 'What a pity you have brought the baby out on such a cold night as this.' At this point, Frances leaned forward and kissed Henry. They all walked on together and, as they approached Ann's house, Frances asked if they might come in for a while.

Inside her home, Ann gave Frances some bread, cheese and ale. Ann had not had any beer in the house so went on to the nearest ale-house to get some. On the way she saw Henrietta Scrivener who told her that she was looking for her child, which Frances had taken without her permission. Thinking that this was nothing more than a domestic dispute, Ann did not tell Henrietta that Frances and the boy were at her house but, when she returned home, she told Frances what Henrietta had said to her and advised her to return home with the child, without delay. Frances replied, 'The boy is all right, bless his heart. He loves his granny and his granny loves him.' Frances left

Lawrence Street some time after 9.00pm, having promised that she was on her way back to Lordship Place.

After Caroline Stewart had given her testimony, Constable Henry Dent told the court that he had gone to Bacon's Hotel and arrested Frances. She was then taken to Bow Street police station but later, after the letter Frances had left for her daughter was handed over, Frances was moved to Chelsea police station, where she was charged with murder.

Inspector James Sherlock was the senior officer on duty at Chelsea. After reading the letter, he showed it to Frances who admitted that she had written it. Inspector Sherlock was also present at the magistrate's hearing on 2 May. After the proceedings had concluded, Frances made a statement to him, which he wrote down in his notebook. In that statement she detailed her movements after leaving Lordship Place and ended by again admitting that she had thrown the baby into the Thames.

Edward King was the next witness. He testified that he had been near the Millwall Docks at around 12.30pm on 2 May, when he had seen something floating in the water. After some difficulty, Edward managed to snare the object and bring it to the bank. Only then did he see that it was the body of a child.

Dr William Giles had examined the body of the child at Poplar mortuary. Later he had performed the post-mortem and confirmed that death was due to drowning. There were no signs of external violence on the body.

In her defence, Frances withdrew her confessions to the murder and now claimed that Henry had fallen into the water accidentally. Under cross-examination, however, she could offer no explanation as to why she had not gone for help or reported the matter to the authorities.

The jury deliberated for just a few minutes before returning their guilty verdict but they did add a strong recommendation to mercy on account of Frances's age and the mental excitement she was under at the time she committed the crime.

That recommendation had no effect. Having been sentenced to death, Frances was hanged, by William Marwood, at Newgate prison, on Monday, 29 June 1874.

Chapter 11

Charles O'Donnell
1876

Charles Christian Scherer lived at 28 Lower George Street, Chelsea and had, until very recently, two lodgers living with him, Charles O'Donnell and his wife, Elizabeth.

At approximately 4.45pm on Sunday, 29 October 1876, Charles O'Donnell paid a visit to his ex-landlord and, after exchanging pleasantries, the two men sat down to a refreshing cup of tea. The conversation, rather naturally, turned to O'Donnell's family and Mr Scherer asked how Elizabeth was. O'Donnell remained silent for a moment and then replied that he hoped she was in Heaven by that time. Mr Scherer thought that O'Donnell might have been drinking and that this was the alcohol talking, so he didn't pursue the matter. O'Donnell, however, had not finished and now asked his friend for a piece of paper. One was handed over and upon it O'Donnell wrote, 'I trust you will see us buried as soon as you can. Pay yourself, and give my respects to your wife and child.'

Charles Scherer was puzzled by what this scrap of paper meant and O'Donnell explained that it was his last will and testament. He was asking his ex-landlord to be his executor, pay himself for his services and then arrange funerals for O'Donnell and his wife. Scherer still thought that this might be the drink talking, but O'Donnell still insisted that his wife was dead and that soon he would be too.

At 6.00pm, O'Donnell stood to leave. The two men shook hands and, as he left, O'Donnell remarked, 'Mr Scherer, I don't suppose you'll see me alive again.' For some time after that, Charles Scherer thought about what O'Donnell had said and then, finally, decided to see if there was any truth in it.

Leaving his own house, Scherer walked to O'Donnell's new lodgings at Rawlings Street, also in Chelsea. There, he spoke to O'Donnell's landlady, told her of his encounter with her tenant, and that he believed that there might be something wrong. To be on the safe side, he was now going to the police station to report the matter.

By 8.00pm, Charles Scherer was back at Rawlings Street but this time he was with Inspector William March. The two men then entered O'Donnell's rooms where they found Elizabeth O'Donnell dead in her bed.

Some ninety minutes later, at 9.30pm, Charles O'Donnell arrived back at Scherer's home in Lower George Street, in a cab. Mr Scherer immediately climbed in next to O'Donnell and escorted him to the police station where he was charged with his wife's murder.

Charles O'Donnell faced his trial on 20 November, where he was defended by Mr Montagu Williams. Mr Poland, assisted by Mr Beasley, outlined the case for the prosecution.

Charles Scherer told the court of O'Donnell's visit to his home on 29 October and confirmed that he and his wife Elizabeth had lived with him, until just before her death.

Inspector March told of his findings when he had entered the room at Rawlings Street. Elizabeth O'Donnell lay in the bed, her head and neck black and discoloured with bruises. There was a large wound over her right eye and the bedclothes were saturated with blood. It was clear that Elizabeth had been battered to death and the weapon used appeared to be a pair of heavy fire tongs. These had been found in a corner of the room and the top of them was covered with blood and hair. The room itself was in a great state of confusion and a number of mirrors had been smashed.

Doctor John Henry Waters had been called to the scene to examine the dead woman. He believed that she had been dead for perhaps three days, meaning that she might have died as early as 26 October. He also believed that Elizabeth had been attacked whilst she was asleep as there were no signs of a struggle around the bed itself.

Ann Wheeler was another lodger at the house in Rawlings Street and she testified that at around 9.40pm on Thursday, 26 October, she had heard Elizabeth call her name several times, from the foot of the stairs. When Ann went to see what she wanted, Elizabeth handed her a parcel and asked her to keep it safe for her. She had not told Ann what it contained and, after Elizabeth had been found dead, Ann handed the parcel to the police. She was present when the parcel was opened and saw that it contained nine £5 notes and three sovereigns, a total of £48 in cash.

Ann was also able to confirm that the O'Donnell's had come to live at Rawlings Street on 14 October. She had grown very close to Elizabeth in the time that she was there and she had told Ann that she had married O'Donnell on 22 December 1874, her maiden name being Elizabeth Sullivan.

Charles O'Donnell had offered no reason for his attack upon his wife, though the hiding of the parcel of money might have suggested that she was frightened that he would possibly spend it on drink. He never denied that he was responsible for Elizabeth's death and, therefore, the only real defence was that he was insane at the time the crime was committed.

Knowing that this would be the defence strategy, the prosecution called Dr John Roland Gibson, the surgeon at Newgate prison. He had observed O'Donnell since 9 November and believed him to be of sound mind. To counter this, the defence called Dr Dover who had previously treated O'Donnell for mental problems. Dr Dover had first examined O'Donnell in May 1875 and believed him to have suicidal tendencies. For that reason, he had him committed to the Colney Hatch asylum from where O'Donnell had been released earlier that year.

In the event, the jury came to believe that O'Donnell was guilty as charged and he was duly sentenced to death. That sentence was carried out at Newgate on 11 December 1876, by William Marwood.

Chapter 12

Michael McConnon
1877

On the evening of Monday, 25 December 1876, Sergeant Charles Shepherd of the 1st Battalion, Grenadier Guards, was not joining in with the Christmas revelries. Shepherd was the duty sergeant in the guardroom at the Chelsea barracks, ready to take in any soldier who had a little too much to drink, or committed some other breach of army rules.

The first man brought in that evening was Private Alfred John Rawlings. He was not arrested for being drunk and disorderly, but for refusing to obey orders. He was placed inside the guardroom, a room with one large wooden bench or bed off to one side, where soldiers could rest. Rawlings wasted little time in lying down and getting off to sleep.

The next soldier to be brought to the guardroom was Private John Slack, who was suffering from the effects of rather too much alcohol. He too found a place on the large bed and began sleeping off the beer.

Some twenty minutes later, Private John Brewerton was marched in. He was sober and had been charged with being absent without leave. Brewerton joined his two fellow prisoners on the bed and he too fell into a deep sleep.

At 11.30pm, a fourth prisoner, Private Noah Johnson, was escorted into the room. Johnson was very drunk and rather dirty, having fallen over in the street. He looked around the room, at the other three prisoners who were all now, apparently, in a deep sleep, and found himself a place on the bed.

Twenty minutes after this, at 11.50pm, two police constables entered the barracks, and flanked by them was a fifth soldier, twenty-four-year-old Private Michael McConnon of the 2nd

Battalion. He, too, was very drunk and, after details of his arrest were given to Sergeant Shepherd, was placed with the other prisoners in the guardroom. Ten minutes after this, at midnight, Sergeant Shepherd glanced through the peephole into the guardroom and saw that all was well. Four men were asleep on the wooden bed and the fifth, McConnon, was sitting on that same bed, away from the other four.

Fifteen minutes later, at 12.15am on Tuesday, 26 December, cries of 'Murder!' rang out from the guardroom. Sergeant Shepherd looked through the peephole again. Now, two men were standing against the far wall, obviously afraid. McConnon was pulling a third man along the floor and the fifth man, Noah Johnson, was nowhere to be seen.

Without further delay, Shepherd opened the door and marched into the guardroom. Now, he could see the fifth man, Johnson, lying off to one side. He was face down and his head was covered in blood. McConnon was placed in a separate lock-up, the other three were moved to a large cell and the doctor called to attend to Johnson. It was all to no avail. Private Johnson was already dead and McConnon found himself facing a charge of murder.

The trial of Michael McConnon took place on 8 January 1877, before Mr Justice Hawkins. The first witness was Sergeant Shepherd, who detailed the arrival of the five men on Christmas night. He also testified that when he first entered the guardroom after the attack, McConnon had shouted, 'Take me to a cell, for I have killed him.' McConnon was indeed confined in a separate cell, but it did little to calm him down. For the next half hour or so he kicked against the cell door and only stopped when Shepherd went into the cell and confiscated his boots.

The other three prisoners in that guardroom were obviously important witnesses and the first of these was John Slack. He had been asleep at the time the attack commenced, but was woken by a loud disturbance. Looking across the room he saw Johnson lying on the floor, with McConnon standing over him, kicking him repeatedly in the head. Suddenly, McConnon stopped and turned towards the bed. Brewerton was still lying down and McConnon grabbed hold of his ankles and pulled him onto the floor shouting, 'If you take this man's part, I will serve you the same.'

John Brewerton told the court that he was in a deep sleep and heard nothing of the attack. He was only woken when he was pulled from the bed and threatened by McConnon.

Alfred John Rawlings had also been asleep when the attack started, but he woke and, seeing what was happening, went to stand against the wall, as far away from McConnon as he could. It was Rawlings who shouted, 'Murder!' two or three times, in order to attract the attention of the duty sergeant.

A history of the two men involved in the attack was supplied by Henry Brown, a private in the 1st Battalion of the Grenadier Guards, the same unit that the dead man had belonged. Brown said he had known Johnson for about four years and they were close friends.

At around 9.00pm on the night of 25 December, Brown and Johnson had gone into a beerhouse on Lower George Street, Chelsea, and enjoyed a few pints together. At 10.35pm, McConnon came into the same public house and he was already very drunk. For no apparent reason, McConnon walked up to Johnson and said, 'You are a bloody liar.' To this, Johnson replied, 'You are the same.' There was, however, no further confrontation and Johnson left the bar soon afterwards, to be followed by McConnon a few minutes later. Brown said that he had no idea what the exchange of insults was about.

Constable Octavius Wheeler was on duty in Commercial Road, Pimlico, at 11.30pm, on 25 December, when he saw McConnon approaching. He was obviously very much the worse for drink and when Wheeler spoke to him McConnon took off his tunic and announced that he would fight him. A small crowd gathered and McConnon extended his invitation, saying that he would fight any man there. Wheeler and another officer then arrested McConnon and escorted him to the Chelsea barracks.

Walter Eason was a lance corporal in the 3rd Battalion of the Grenadiers and he was on duty with Sergeant Shepherd at the barracks. He confirmed that Johnson and McConnon were both very drunk when they were brought in.

Sergeant Joseph Thompson had been called to the scene by Sergeant Shepherd, and saw the body of Johnson lying in the guardroom. He then went to McConnon's cell and told him that the man he had attacked was dead, and he would be charged with wilful murder. To this McConnon replied simply, 'I don't care.'

The final witness was Dr Albert Louis Fernandez, the surgeon of the 3rd Battalion, who was called to examine Johnson in the guardroom. He confirmed that the man was dead and two days later, on 28 December, performed the post-mortem. He found Johnson's right ear had been almost kicked from his head. There were three ribs broken on the right side and one of these had lacerated the liver, which was the direct cause of death.

Having listened to the evidence, the jury had no difficulty in deciding that McConnon was guilty, spending just five minutes on their deliberations. McConnon was then sentenced to death by the judge. He did not, however, lose his life in the execution chamber. In due course, the death sentence was respited and McConnon was sent to prison instead.

Chapter 13

The Murder of George James
1878

On the evening of Saturday, 9 January 1878, William Turnbull was making his way home, along Westmoreland Street. Continuing on his journey, William drew near to the railway arch of the Grosvenor Road station, when he heard someone moaning, followed immediately by a single cry of, 'Police!'

Walking gingerly towards the darkened railway arch, William saw a man lying on the ground and a second man standing over him, striking him repeatedly on the head. William called out and this seemed to frighten the assailant for he immediately ran off into the night. William bravely gave chase but, after some 200 yards or so, lost his quarry. William ran on towards Chelsea Bridge where he found Constable Alfred Nichols. He quickly explained to the officer what had happened and the two men then went back to where the victim of the attack had lain.

The stricken man still lay close to the railway arch and was moving about, obviously in pain. Constable Nichols asked him who he was and what had happened to him. The man did reply but his voice was low and slurred and Nichols could not understand what he said.

Turnbull and Nichols helped the man to his feet and helped him to take a few steps but it was plain that he was in no condition to walk further. A cab was called and the man taken to St George's Hospital where he was attended to by Mr Tidswell. A quick examination showed that the victim had a compressed fracture of the skull and would need an immediate operation. The operation was carried out that same night but soon afterwards, inflammation set in. Nine days later, on 18 January, Mr Tidswell's patient died.

Police enquiries soon revealed that the dead man's name was George James and he lodged at 58 Welling Street. His landlady, Mary Ann Anslow, told officers that Mr James had left the house on the evening of 9 January, to visit his niece. At the time, George had a parcel of clothing with him. Mrs Anslow was also able to say that her tenant habitually carried a gold watch and chain and wore two heavy gold rings on his fingers.

George James had been on his way to Camberwell. John Dixon, of 131 Bell Street, in that township, stated that the dead man was his wife's uncle. George had been fifty-six years old at the time of his death, and he never arrived at their house on the night in question.

Both Constable Nichols and Mr Tidswell, the surgeon, testified that no parcel or money had been found on George James, but he still wore his gold watch and chain, and the two rings. It was clear that robbery had been the motive for the attack but it also seemed that William Turnbull's arrival on the scene had disturbed the thief who had not had time to steal the other items.

The inquest on George James took place at St George's Hospital, on 22 February, before the coroner, Mr Bedford. Not surprisingly, having listened to the various witnesses, the jury had little alternative but to return a verdict of 'murder by person or persons unknown'.

Despite William Turnbull being able to give a rough description of the man he had chased away from the railway arch, the assailant was never found and the murder of George James remains unsolved.

Chapter 14

Henry Perry
1880

Mr Barham, a grocer, operated three shops across London. One, at 3 Raven Row, Spitalfields, which he owned outright, but he was also a partner in the other two. In shops at 14 Aldersgate Street and 70 High Street, Kensington, Barham was in partnership with James Marriage. By all accounts, all three shops were quite successful.

As far as the shops at Aldersgate Street and High Street were concerned, it was company policy, each Saturday, to combine the takings of the two premises. In order to achieve this, one of the young apprentices would be sent first to the shop in Kensington, where he would collect the money from the tills, and would take this, travelling, via the underground, to the shop in Aldersgate Street, where he would hand the takings over to the manager. On Saturday, 21 August 1880, this duty fell to eighteen-year-old Clarence Lewis.

It was around 11.00pm when Lewis entered the ticket office at Kensington station. As he queued patiently for his ticket, a man grabbed him by the arm. Lewis pulled away, looked at the stranger with disdain and told him that he must be some sort of lunatic to simply grab hold of someone in that manner. Having paid for his ticket, Lewis then went on to the platform, followed by the man who had accosted him.

As Lewis waited for his train, the man approached him again and asked, 'Don't you know me?' Lewis replied that he did not, whereupon the man continued, 'I am Perry that used to be at Aldersgate, and I thought you were too proud to speak to me.' Lewis thought for a moment and then realised that this was a man he vaguely recognised, as one who had served behind the counter at the Aldersgate Street shop.

The two men then fell into conversation and, at one stage, Perry asked Lewis what kind of ticket he had purchased. Lewis replied that he had bought a third-class return ticket. Perry said his was a first-class one and asked Lewis if he would ride with him in first class. If he did, then Perry would be happy to pay the excess fare. Lewis agreed and, when the train pulled into the platform, the two men climbed in to an otherwise deserted first-class compartment.

The train had not been moving for very long when Perry stood up and looked over a low partition that divided their compartment from the next. He then produced a small bottle, which he said was a non-alcoholic tonic, and invited Lewis to take a sip. Rather foolishly perhaps, Lewis took a sip and found that the liquid tasted foul. As he handed the bottle back to Perry, Lewis began to feel a little drowsy.

If anything, Perry's behaviour then became even more strange. He now produced a handkerchief, poured some of the liquid from the bottle onto it, and invited Lewis to smell it. At first, Lewis refused but Perry then placed the handkerchief against Lewis's nose. Lewis thought it better to humour his companion and pretended to sniff the material but actually held his breath.

After a few minutes, Perry removed the handkerchief and Lewis turned his head away. Almost immediately, Perry struck Lewis a severe blow on the head with his walking stick. A dazed Lewis fell from his seat onto the carriage floor where further blows were rained down upon his head.

When the train pulled into a station, Perry leapt upon Lewis, placing his knees on the injured man's chest and clamping a hand over his mouth so that he could not call out for help. Lewis pulled free and cried, 'Murder!' but no one seemed to hear. At that Perry placed his hands around Lewis's throat and tried to strrangle him. Then, as the train pulled out of the station, Perry let his victim go but then started hitting him again with the stick. At one stage Lewis managed to crawl part of the way under a seat so that now his head was protected. It did nothing to stop the furious attack upon him and Perry now struck him about the shoulders and upper body.

Finally, the brutal attack stopped. For a few seconds, Lewis lay on the carriage floor, before turning over to see that his assailant had left. The train had stopped at another station and Perry had left the compartment. Pulling himself painfully to his feet, Lewis saw his attacker strolling down the platform, his walking stick in one hand and a parcel in the other. That parcel contained the money which Lewis was taking to the Aldersgate Street branch.

Lewis managed, somehow, to stagger onto the platform and stagger after Perry. There was no way he was able to catch his attacker so Lewis called out, 'Stop this man. He has taken my money and knocked me about.' To his relief, as he fell to the station floor, Lewis saw a number of men seize hold of Perry, before he slipped into unconsciousness.

Henry Perry had been taken by some members of the public and some of the station staff, and given over to police custody. Though he had denied any attack upon Clarence Lewis, he had been charged with violently assaulting him and made his first appearance before the magistrate on Monday, 23 August.

This initial appearance took place at the Guildhall Police Court. Details of the charge were read out and it was suggested that this would later be amended to one of attempted murder. The court was told that the injured man was now in a serious condition in St Bartholomew's Hospital and was far too ill to attend court at this stage.

The court was also informed that Perry had, indeed, once worked at the Aldersgate Street branch and so knew the routine about combining the takings from the two shops, though he had never been asked to do this himself. Perry had worked at the shop from March 1879 up to April 1880, when he had been dismissed.

The Saturday in question had been the first time that Clarence Lewis had carried out the task of collecting the money. On the previous three Saturdays, the money had been collected by an apprentice named Frederick Emmett and on each occasion, Perry had been at Kensingon station, waiting for Emmett. Each time he had spoken with Emmett and each time he had travelled on the railway with him. This suggested that the crime had been planned over a number of weeks.

The only witness was Constable Joseph Eve, who gave details of Perry's arrest. Eve testified that it had been approximately 11.07pm, when he had been called to the Aldersgate Street station on the Metropolitan railway. He found Perry being held by a railway constable and a gentleman named John Bell. Perry had a parcel in his right hand and Eve had taken this and handed it to his inspector at the police station. He was present when this parcel was opened and saw that it contained two cheques for £8 each, seven £5 banknotes, £58 10s in gold and some lesser coin. The total amount in the parcel was £104 14s 1d and it had been confirmed that this was the money from the shop in Kensington.

Perry had been searched at the station and two small bottles, containing liquid, were discovered. One of these seemed to contain port wine, whilst the other held chloroform, but these had been handed to a chemist for proper examination. After Perry had been charged, Eve returned to the railway station and found a heavy walking stick in a recess behind an advertisement board. The stick had blood and hair adhering to one end.

After this testimony had been heard, the proceedings were adjourned until Friday, 27 August. On that date, the prosecution opened the proceedings by stating that it had now become clear that Perry had given his real name to Lewis, before the attack. Had this been a simple robbery, he would have certainly been caught when those details were passed on to the police. This, in turn, suggested that Perry had intended that Lewis should not survive the attack upon him and, for that reason, the charge was now changed to one of attempted murder.

Another policeman was the first witness at this second hearing. Constable Henry Hird was a railway policeman, working for the Metropolitan Railway. He had been at the Aldersgate Street station when a train pulled in at 11.06pm. Hird saw a crowd of people at one end of the platform, and some sort of disturbance, so went to investigate. On arrival at the far end he saw Lewis, bleeding badly from a head wound, lying on the platform. Perry stood nearby, being held by John Bell and a porter. The prisoner had a parcel in his hand and at first claimed that it was his property. He claimed that the injured man was a friend of his and that he had had nothing to do with any attack upon him. Perry suggested that his friend may have fallen over inside the carriage.

Alfred Stickley was the station inspector and he had been standing around the middle of the platform as the train pulled in. Just as the train was about to leave, Stickley heard a cry from the far end of the platform. Going to see what the problem was, Stickley found Lewis being supported by some members of the public. He was only semi-conscious but managed to say that Perry had attacked him and stolen his money. Stickley asked for more information and Lewis managed to gasp out, 'We were coming in a first-class carriage together and he tried to give me laudanum or poison, and he tried to chloroform me, and afterwards tried to murder me by beating me over the head with a stick.'

John Bell was a bricklayer by trade and, on the day in question, was at the station with his brother, Thomas. The train pulled into the station and almost immediately John heard someone calling 'Stop thief!' or something similar. Turning they saw Perry, strolling along the platform with a walking stick in one hand and a parcel in the other. It had been Thomas who ran after Perry and seized him. Perry began to struggle violently and John went to his brother's aid. As they held him, Perry tried to throw the parcel onto the railway line but Thomas prevented him from doing so. This evidence was confirmed by the next witness, Thomas Bell himself.

Lewis Watson was a porter at the station and he testified that he had helped John Bell to hold on to Perry, once he had been seized. He was followed to the stand by James Marriage, the partner in the grocery shops, who confirmed that Perry had once worked at the Spitalfields shop, which was run by his partner.

Frederick Emmett was the apprentice who had collected the money from the Kensington shop on the three Saturdays before the attack. He confirmed that each time Perry, who he knew well from the time he had worked at the shop, was waiting for him. On the second Saturday, Perry had tried to get him to take a drink of what looked like port wine, but he had refused and in a temper, Perry threw the bottle out of the carriage window.

The two bottles taken from Perry had been given to Otto Hehner, a Fellow of the Chemical Society, for examination. He confirmed that one contained pure chloroform whilst the other held port wine, which had been dosed with a liberal amount of laudanum.

Dr Walter Griffiths was the house surgeon at St Bartholomew's Hospital and he detailed the injuries Lewis had suffered. There were a large number of wounds on his head and they could have been inflicted by the walking stick found at the station. There was no way that such injuries could have been sustained by a fall in a railway carriage.

One more adjournment followed, to Monday, 26 August. On that date, the only witness called was Clarence Lewis who was, by now, out of the hospital. After he had given his evidence, Perry was sent for trial on two charges: robbery and attempted murder.

Perry's trial took place on 15 September, before Mr Justice Stephen. Mr Poland and Mr Montagu Williams appeared for the prosecution, and Perry was defended by Mr Greer and Mr Morice. All the evidence previously detailed was heard again and the jury took just a few minutes to return a verdict of guilty of both charges. The sentence given was that Perry must suffer thirty lashes from a cat-o'-nine-tails and then serve twenty years in prison. Perry screamed as the sentence was announced.

In the days that followed, a number of people wrote to the newspapers, expressing their views on the sentence. Many wrote that the sentence was well deserved. Some of the more humane writers stated that they believed that thirty lashes were much too severe and that a mere twenty-four might have been better!

Chapter 15

Robert Booley
1883

Frances Croft lived at 31 Gertrude Street, Kensington, and made a living by taking in lodgers. In 1883, she had three ladies living with her: Minnie Clayton, Hetty Castleton and Blanche Lowry, who preferred to use the name 'Jennie'.

One of those three lodgers, Hetty Castleton, earned her living as a prostitute and in the early hours of Wednesday, 2 May 1883, she returned home with a client. They were admitted to the house by Blanche, and went into the drawing room. Almost immediately there was a loud knock on the front door.

It was Frances herself who went to the door this time. A man she knew as Robert James Booley then pushed past her without so much as a word and stormed into the drawing room. Booley was a regular client of Hetty's and it seemed he was not too pleased with the fact that she was now with another man.

Strong words passed between Booley and Hetty, during which her potential client thought better of things and ran out of the house. Satisfied that he had achieved what he desired, Booley then began to leave the house himself. Frances was still in the hallway and another argument then followed between her and Booley, during which she told him what she thought of him barging into her home.

The argument grew ever more heated and Frances, not one to mince her words, used some rather foul language towards her unwanted visitor. Still not satisfied that she had done enough, Frances then lashed out and struck Booley on the face. He immediately hit her back and a brief scuffle followed. Meanwhile, Hetty Castleton ran after her potential client, caught up with him across the road, and began trying to persuade him to return to the house.

Booley was a cabman by trade and he now stormed out of the house and climbed into his cab, which was standing outside. He only moved the cab to the corner of Gertrude Street though, where he stopped, no doubt to cool off a little. If he thought, however, that he would now be left in peace, he was very much mistaken. Hetty was having no luck in persuading her gentleman to return to number 31 with her, so she marched up to Booley to let him know what she thought of him.

Having given Booley a piece of her mind, Hetty Castleton returned to number 31 where she found the front door locked, Frances Croft lying on a grass verge outside and Blanche Lowry trying to lift her. By this time, Minnie Clifton had also gone to speak to Booley about his behaviour and they were still on the corner of Gertrude Street. Hetty went back to the corner of the street, told Minnie that Frances had fallen over and asked her to return and help her to lift the stricken woman. Minnie did as she was asked and, when it was clear that Frances could not be roused, ran off to fetch the doctor. However, when the doctor did attend, he found that Frances Croft was dead. The police were called and Booley was taken into custody, where he was charged with manslaughter.

Booley's trial on that charge took place on 28 May. His defence lay in the hands of Mr Strong, whilst the case for the prosecution was led by Mr Poland, assisted by Mr Montagu Williams and Mr A E Gill.

After Hetty Castleton had given her testimony, Blanche Lowry took the stand. She had heard the scuffle in the hallway and heard Frances call Booley a brute, for hitting an old woman. After Booley had left the house, Blanche had seen him park his cab on the corner of Gertrude Street and, after Hetty had had words with him, Blanche went to talk to him too. Booley had obviously had enough by this time, for he informed her that if she rounded on him, he would 'smash her face in'.

Minnie Clayton told the court that she had only moved into the house at 31 Gertrude Street on Friday 27 April. After the arguments, she had also gone to speak to Booley. Moments later, Hetty Castleton had come back to the cab and said, 'Minnie, come, I think my landlady is in a fit.' Minnie had gone back to find Frances lying on a grass verge, close to her front door. When it was clear that she would not wake, Minnie ran for the doctor. Later, after the doctor had said that Frances was dead, Hetty had also run off to find a policeman.

Emily Jenner lived at 31 Limerston Street, but on 2 May, she was walking down Gertrude Street with her friend, Norah Burton. Emily had seen some sort of heated discussion taking place between Booley and some women on the corner of the street. She and Norah then walked on together and, when they came opposite to number 31, they saw Frances lying on the grass. She was doubled up and had blood on her face. This was confirmed by Norah, who added that she had touched Frances's legs and found them to be quite cold.

Constable Horace Thorpe was the policeman brought to the scene by Hetty Castleton. He had found Frances lying on her stomach, on the grass. There was a great deal of blood around her mouth.

Inspector William Demain had seen Frances's body and at 5.00am that same morning, he had gone to Booley's lodgings at 89 Aldersgate Street and arrested him. Later, at the Chelsea police station, Demain had charged Booley with murder. Another inspector, Patrick Cronin, was present at the time and he heard Booley reply, 'I did not strike her and knock her down.' Later, at the magistrates' court, the charge was reduced to one of manslaughter as it was believed that there had been no intention to kill.

Lucy Haynes was Frances Croft's niece and she confirmed that Frances had been sixty-two years old when she died. Lucy was also able to confirm that Frances had never suffered from fits of any kind, thus closing off one possible line of defence for Robert Booley.

Dr James Robert Hayes had examined Frances in Gertrude Street and believed that she had been dead for about an hour when he arrived. Later, Dr Hayes performed the post-mortem and he found an effusion of blood beneath the skull. The brain had been compressed and such an injury could be caused by either a sharp blow, or, just possibly, a fall.

Once all the evidence had been heard, the jury took just a few minutes to decide that the defendant was guilty of manslaughter. Twenty-eight-year-old Robert James Booley was then sentenced to eighteen months' imprisonment, with hard labour.

Chapter 16

Henry (Harry) John Surtees
1883

The night of Friday, 29 June 1883, was absolutely foul. Great peals of thunder and sheets of lightning ran across the skies and the rain bounced off the pavements. Inside the *World's End* public house on King's Road, Chelsea, groups of people huddled around the fire, enjoying their drinks and marvelling at the awful weather outside.

In due course, the time came for customers to leave but the rain still pelted down and as people drifted outside, many of them took shelter in the stable yard at the back of the pub. One such person was James Gallimore who, as he pulled his coat up around his chin, saw a number of people he knew, taking shelter at the far end of the same stable yard.

Amongst that group were Samuel Bell, a cab driver, and a man named Carter who were trying to coax a somewhat reluctant horse out of the stables, so that Bell could attach the beast to his cab, which stood in the street outside. Also there were Harry John Surtees and Louisa Charlotte Parrell, who Gallimore had seen leave the bar just a few minutes before he had.

Even as Gallimore sheltered he saw Surtees pick up a pail of water and throw it over Louisa. According to his later testimony, which did not agree with that of others who witnessed this scene, Surtees then refilled the pail and threw it over Louisa again before repeating this for a third time. Surtees then struck Louisa in the throat, knocking her back into the stable.

Gallimore dashed forward and shouted, 'Leave off, you have done quite enough Harry.' At first it seemed that Surtees had heeded Gallimore's words for he then helped Louisa up, but no sooner had she stood up than he struck her a second time, knocking her backwards again.

Other people, including Elizabeth Dorrington, who was a close friend of Louisa's, now rushed to aid the stricken woman. Louisa was helped up again and she was then helped to her lodgings at 59 Langton Street. As the group moved along the streets, they were followed by Surtees, who had picked up Louisa's hat and cloak and was carrying them over his arm.

Susan Davidson was Louisa's landlady at Langton Street and she heard a noisy group bringing Louisa in, taking her to her room and putting her to bed. Susan noticed that Louisa was very wet indeed and appeared to be in some pain as she was groaning and moaning. Susan also saw Surtees, who she knew had been walking out with Louisa, and asked him if he had hit her. Surtees replied that they had been sheltering in the stable and a horse must have kicked her. Hearing this, Louisa managed to groan, 'Oh Harry, you know what you have done.'

By the next morning, 30 June, Louisa was no better and it was decided that she had to go to the hospital. Another lodger at number 59, Elizabeth Weedon, helped Louisa to get dressed and she helped Surtees to take the injured woman to St George's Hospital. Surtees, however, refused to go inside and left Elizabeth to escort Louisa to see the doctor. When Elizabeth came back outside, Surtees did not seem too interested in what the doctor had said, inquiring only what Louisa might have told him. Elizabeth replied, 'The truth, that you had kicked her.'

On Monday, 2 July, having received an official complaint from Louisa, Inspector Henry Marshall arrested Surtees at his mother's house at 9 Sloane Square. He was charged with violent assault or wounding and held in custody to await a hearing before the magistrates. Unfortunately, the following day, Tuesday, 3 July, Louisa died from her injuries and the charge of murder was added to that of wounding. Later, at the inquest, that charge was amended, to one of manslaughter.

Surtees' trial took place on 30 July and he faced three separate charges. In addition to manslaughter and wounding he was now also charged with breaking the peace.

After James Gallimore had given his evidence, the prosecution called Samuel Bell, the cab driver. He testified that he had been taking care of his horse when Louisa came into the stable. She was obviously the worse for drink and staggered to the corn bin where she took a handful of corn and fed it to the horse. Minutes later, Surtees had also come into the stable and an argument had started between then. At one stage, Louisa had rushed forward to grab at Surtees and it was at that point that the prisoner had thrown a single pail of water over her. This did nothing to cool Louisa's temper and she rushed at Surtees again. It was then that he struck her a single blow and she fell back against the corn bin.

Frederick Mason was also standing in the stable and he heard a little more of the argument between Surtees and Louisa. He had, apparently, accused her of going with a married man and at one stage called her 'a cow'. She replied by calling Surtees 'a sod' and hitting him in the side of his head. Mason did not see Surtees hit Louisa but claimed that he had simply pushed her backwards.

Doctor William Rivers Pollock had attended to Louisa when she was brought in to St George's Hospital, at 11.00am on 30 June. She seemed to be quite ill and complained of acute pains in her abdomen. Soon afterwards, Dr Pollock had gone off duty and Dr Henry William Allingham had taken over Louisa's care. He was present when she died, at 5.20pm, on 3 July.

Yet another medical gentleman, Dr Daniel Maclure Ross, had performed the post-mortem, on 4 July and he found that Louisa's bladder had been ruptured. This had caused peritonitis, which was the direct cause of death. The damage to the bladder may have been caused by a punch or a kick but could equally have been caused by a fall against the corn bin in the stable.

The medical evidence, and the conflicting testimony of the various witnesses, some of who had seen a blow, others of whom had only seen a push, meant that the jury returned a not guilty verdict on the charge of manslaughter. The prosecution then chose not to enter any evidence on the other two charges, which were then dismissed. Harry John Surtees then walked from court, a free man.

Chapter 17

Samuel Davis and
Alfred George Plank
1885

The evening of 2 December 1885, had been a busy one in the *Clock House Tavern,* in Knightsbridge. The potman, Edward Tilley, had been run off his feet most of the night but, by 11.00pm, the rush seemed to have died down somewhat, and only a few customers stayed behind, finishing off their drinks.

At 11.15pm, three soldiers, Harry Denton, Thomas Cooper and Samuel Lockwood, walked into the bar. All three men were members of the Coldstream Guards and all wore medals on their chests. No sooner had they ordered their drinks, than three local men, Samuel Davis, Alfred George Plank and Joseph Philip Hawkes, stepped forward and began goading the three men in uniform.

Hawkes took little part in the banter and it seemed to be Davis who did most of the talking. He told the three soldiers that they had not earned their medals and had no business wearing them. The soldiers told him to mind his own business and pointed out that they had only come in for a quiet drink and did not want any trouble. This did nothing to calm Davis down and he then took out his coat and said that he would fight all, or any of them.

At this provocation, Edward Tilley stepped around the bar and told Davis to clear off and take his two friends with him. When Davis stood firm, Tilley manhandled him out of the bar, into the street outside. As Davis shouted abuse from the street, and threatened what he would do, Plank and Hawkes calmly followed their friend outside.

Edward Tilley went back to his duties and served the three soldiers with their drinks. Peace only reigned for a minute or so, though, for then Davis stormed back in, without his coat, grabbed hold of the nearest soldier, which happened to be Thomas Cooper, and tried to pull him out into the street so that they could fight. Once again, Edward Tilley intervened and, once again, Davis was thrown out.

The soldiers finished their drinks and left the tavern together a few minutes later. All three walked down to the corner of Sloane Street, where they all shook hands and bade each other goodnight. Cooper was only on a one-night pass and had to report back to his barracks. The other two, Denton and Lockwood, both had extended passes and were free to go elsewhere. After the handshakes were completed, Denton and Lockwood walked off towards Piccadilly and Cooper carried on down Sloane Street.

Denton and Lockwood had not gone very far when a figure dashed out from behind a corner. Denton knew nothing more as a punch under his jaw knocked him down to the ground. It was a local constable who came to Denton's aid, picked him up, dusted him down and then watched as he and Lockwood went on their way.

The assailant had, of course, been Samuel Davis and he was still with his friend, Alfred Plank. They saw the policeman approaching and wasted no time in making good their getaway down Sloane Street, chasing after Cooper as they did so.

Adam Storey was a private in the 1st Battalion of the Coldstream Guards and he too was returning to barracks and walking down Sloane Street. Storey noticed Cooper, who was in the same battalion and whom he knew well, walking on the opposite side of the street. As Storey started to cross the road to join his comrade, two men rushed up to Cooper and one of the men struck him savagely behind his right ear. Cooper fell to the ground and Storey made an attempt to grab the man who had hit him, but he managed to struggle free and Storey watched helplessly as both men then ran off. It was Storey's cries for help, which brought a constable to the scene.

Thomas Cooper was rushed to St George's Hospital, but despite the best medical attention, he died the following morning, without ever regaining consciousness. Police enquiries at the *Clock House Tavern* soon led to positive identification of the three men who had goaded the soldiers and Davis, Plank and Hawkes were all arrested and charged with murder. In the event, once the three made their appearance before the magistrates, all charges against Hawkes were dropped, as it was accepted that he had taken no part in the attack itself. Further, the charges against the other two were amended to ones of manslaughter, the magistrates believing that there had been no actual intention to kill.

The trial of Davis and Plank took place on 14 December, with Mr Poland and Mr Montagu Williams detailing the case for the Crown. Davis was defended by Mr Keith Frith, whilst Plank was represented by Mr Geoghegan.

After Edward Tilley had given his testimony, Harry Denton, the soldier who had been battered to the ground, told the court his story. He confirmed that he and his two friends had gone into the *Clock House* at around 11.15pm and immediately been met by abuse from the two prisoners, chiefly from Davis. After he had recovered from the blow on the corner of Sloane Street, he and Lockwood had walked on to Piccadilly. He saw nothing of the attack upon Cooper.

Samuel Lockwood had actually seen neither the attack upon Cooper nor the one upon Denton. Lockwood had walked a few steps ahead of Denton and, after hearing a cry, turned to see him lying on the ground. A policeman then came forward and helped his friend to his feet, before sending them on their way.

Daniel Parrott was a butler, in service at 42 Prince's Gardens, Kensington, but on 2 December, at some time between 11.00pm and midnight, he was walking past the *Clock House Tavern* when he saw a slight scuffle in the doorway. This was, apparently, Edward Tilley, in the act of ejecting Davis from the premises, for the second time. Plank was standing a few yards away and Parrott heard him say something like, 'Wait a minute, until they get round the corner.'

Soon after this, Parrott saw three soldiers come out of the tavern and walk towards Sloane Street. Though he did not know the man at the time, Parrott then saw Davis run from around a corner and strike Denton before he and Plank ran off up Sloane Street, towards Cooper. Parrott, concerned that a serious assault had already been committed, ran after the two men. Moments later, he saw Cooper lying on the pavement and ran on to find a constable.

Constable Thomas Thomas had been on duty that night and at around 11.30pm he saw Davis outside the *Clock House*, threatening someone inside. Constable Thomas went up to Davis and told him to clear off. He then went inside the tavern and advised the soldiers to drink up and be on their way. They did as he suggested and, having spoken to the potman for a minute or so, Thomas went back outside to see Denton lying on the ground and Davis standing over him, ready to strike him again. As the officer went to Denton's aid, Davis and Plank ran off.

Just a few moments after this, the last witness, Daniel Parrott, rushed up to Thomas and told him that there was another soldier lying badly injured in Sloane Street. Parrott took Thomas to where the injured man lay and, acting on Thomas's instructions, went off to find another constable who might assist.

This second officer was Constable George Barley who, when he arrived at the scene, saw Cooper still lying unconscious on the pavement. There was blood pouring from his ear. Barley and Thomas then helped take the injured man to hospital.

Doctor Harry Marmaduke was the surgeon on duty at St George's Hospital and he testified that Cooper was brought in just before midnight on 2 December. Despite receiving immediate treatment, he never woke and died at 1.40am on 3 December. Dr Marmaduke later performed the post-mortem and reported a fractured skull with corresponding laceration of the brain.

The jury retired to consider their verdict and, after a short consultation, returned verdicts on both men. Samuel Davis, the man who had undoubtedly struck the blow that killed Cooper, was found guilty of manslaughter and sentenced to five years' imprisonment. Alfred George Plank was found not guilty of manslaughter but was adjudged to be guilty as an accessory to the crime. For that, he received a sentence of fifteen months' hard labour.

Chapter 18

James White
1888

Catherine White enjoyed the trip with her mother, Margaret. It was the morning of Saturday, 3 March 1888 and Catherine had accompanied sixty-seven-year-old Margaret to a house in Balham with some boots her father, James, had repaired. The sum of twelve shillings in payment was handed over and the two ladies then headed back towards Margaret's home, 1 Eden Place, Chelsea.

Before going back to the house, however, Margaret and Catherine enjoyed a glass of gin and some bread and cheese at the *Star and Garter* public house, so it was 12.30pm by the time they arrived at Eden Place.

Catherine's father was sitting on a bench and announced that he would like a pint of beer. It was plain that he had already consumed a good deal of alcohol and Margaret said, 'James, I think you have had enough already. Where did you get it?' James would only reply, 'I have taken a little job home and spent the money.'

Upon hearing that, Margaret White began to cry uncontrollably. The statement from James was symptomatic of all that was wrong with their relationship. James was a skilled shoemaker and had the potential to earn a good living from his trade, but he would much rather do the minimum amount of work and spend the money on drink. He was losing customers on a regular basis and the household income had fallen to almost nothing.

It was clear that James would not be moved from his determination to have his pint of beer so, against her better judgement, Margaret handed him two pence. James left the house immediately and returned a few minutes later with a large flagon of beer. He poured a glass for his wife and then drank the rest himself. He then told his wife and daughter that he did not feel very well and was going to lie down. It was his daughter, Catherine, who saw him to his bed and covered him over with a greatcoat.

When Catherine went back downstairs she found that her mother was crying again, and saying that there were some boots that James was supposed to have mended but he hadn't bothered and so now they wouldn't be paid. There was, however, little that Catherine could do about this. She had to get back to her own home and her husband, David, so she kissed her mother and said she would call back later that evening to make sure that everything was all right.

Margaret and James White had a second married daughter, Fanny Spinks, who lived with her husband and her nine-year-old son, Thomas James Spinks. Later that same day, at some time between 2.00pm and 2.30pm, Thomas Spinks called at his grandparent's house to give Margaret some money from his mother.

When Thomas arrived, he found his grandfather asleep on his bed and his grandmother sitting on a chair in the front room. After handing over the money, Thomas went out to play in the street but very soon afterwards, James White called him in and asked him to make some tea. As Thomas did as his grandfather had asked, James turned to Margaret and asked her for some bread. She replied that there was none in the house and, because he had done little work, there was no money to buy any. James immediately seized hold of his wife and threw her off the chair and onto the floor where she hit her head against a table. Little Thomas, fearful of what he had seen, ran to Johannah Healy's house, at number 1A.

Thomas didn't really have to tell Mrs Healey what was going on as she could plainly hear the argument from next door. She told Thomas to run off and find a constable and in a few minutes, the boy found Constable William Swinden, who was on duty in Fulham Road. The officer went back to Eden Place and warned James White not to disturb the peace any further. At the time, Margaret White was still lying on the floor and the constable believed that she might well be drunk. He chose not to interfere further and did not make any examination of Margaret, to see if she was injured in any way. Soon after this, Thomas Spinks left Eden Place to return home.

At 3.15pm, there was another visitor to the Whites' home at Eden Place. Rebecca Robson lived at 66 Sidney Street and she had left some boots with James, to be mended. When she arrived, Rebecca saw that Margaret White was still lying on the floor, close to the table but now, she was quite naked, apart from a thin black boddice. James was lying on his bed and Rebecca heard him mutter something like, 'I suppose there will be no more work done today.' He then shouted out for his wife to get up and, when she did not move, he jumped from the bed, picked up a poker from the fireplace and made to strike his wife with it.

It was at that point that Rebecca Robson knocked loudly on the open door to attract James's attention. He turned and saw his visitor for the first time, and asked her to come in. This, however, did nothing to dissuade James from his intended course of action for, even as he spoke, he landed a tremendous blow on Margaret, with the poker.

Rebecca cried, 'Oh, have mercy and don't hit the poor creature with the poker.' James replied, 'I don't care if I kill her.' Rebecca turned and said that she was going to find a policeman. She then left and returned home. Rather surprisingly, in view of what she had witnessed, since Rebecca did not see a policeman on her way, she did not bother to report the matter at all.

At 4.30pm, James White was knocking on the front door of another neighbour, Louisa Mayhew, who lived at 4 Eden Place. James explained that he wanted her help to get his wife onto the bed. Louisa went to James's house and found Margaret still lying on the floor, her clothing having seemingly been torn from her. She helped James to put his wife on the bed and he then left the house to get himself some more beer. Louisa then went to her own house to tell her husband, Walter, what she had seen.

By this time, Thomas Spinks had arrived home and told his mother that his grandfather had hit his grandmother. Fanny

Spinks then went to Eden Place herself, taking Thomas with her. They arrived at about 6.00pm and, after seeing Margaret lying on the bed, went to fetch the doctor.

Doctor Daniel Lehaine arrived at Eden Place within the hour, but by then, Margaret White was dead. James was back in his house now and, once the doctor had made his examination, asked if his wife were dead. Told that she was, James replied, 'A bloody good job too. Fetch me my coat and I will go to the police station.'

In fact, James did not leave the house as he had said. It was Dr Lehaine who called at the police station to report what he had seen and some time afterwards, Constable William Davey arrived to take James into custody. He readily admitted that he had struck his wife three times with the poker and, on the way to the station stated, 'We have lived happily together for forty-one years, but if she had done as I told her, I should not have killed her.'

James was charged with murder by Inspector Charles Ross at the King's Road police station and, when asked if he had anything he wished to say, replied, 'She came home drunk, and laid down on the floor. I tried all I could to persuade her to lay down on the bed, and I pulled all the clothes off her, and beat her with the poker. That is how she got killed. When she would not get up, I beat her on the head and body with the poker. I am sorry for it now, but it was done in the heat of passion.'

James White's trial took place on 23 April. In addition to the evidence already detailed, Dr Lehaine, who had performed the post-mortem, was able to report that Margaret's skull was badly fractured and the wounds would have required at least two heavy blows with the knob end of the poker found at the scene. He was also able to tell the court that when he first arrived at Eden Place, James had threatened him and said he would attack him with the same poker.

The guilty verdict was little more than a formality, though the jury did add a strong recommendation to mercy on account of James's age and the fact that the crime did not appear to be premeditated. Despite that, the statutory death sentence was intoned but, eventually, the recommendation was taken into account and James's sentence was commuted to one of imprisonment.

Chapter 19

John Thomas Lawrence
1890

Mary Ann Morgan lived in a room on the top floor of 59 Lower North Street, Chelsea. There were other lodgers in the house and, on the ground floor, lived John Thomas Lawrence and his wife Sophia, who ran a shop, which sold meat for cats.

On Thursday, 20 February 1890, Mary Ann returned home from her work at around noon and, as she walked up the stairs, she passed the rooms of the Lawrences. As she did so, Mary Ann heard Sophia say, 'You had better kill me at once you brute.' This was followed by the sounds of scuffling, and a thud.

At approximately 12.20pm, John Lawrence shouted for Mary Ann Morgan to come down, saying that he wanted her help. Mary Ann duly descended the stairs but, when she reached the ground floor, she found Lawrence, who was extremely drunk, supporting himself on the banisters. As for Sophia, she lay on her back at the foot of the staircase.

Mary Ann demanded to know what Lawrence had done, but he simply told her that it was none of her business. He then demanded that Mary Ann help him get his wife to bed. Fearful, perhaps, that she might be the next target of his temper, Mary Ann helped Lawrence to get his wife to their bedroom, but before they could put the injured woman onto her bed, Lawrence left the room, leaving Mary Ann to manage things herself.

There was no way that Mary Ann Morgan could get Sophia to bed without further assistance, so she called for help and Mrs Hilsden, another lodger, came to her aid. Together the two women managed to manoeuvre Sophia to bed, where they undressed her. To their horror they discovered that Sophia, who was very pregnant at the time, was bleeding badly from her lower parts. Mary Ann wasted no time in calling out the doctor.

Dr William John Frankish arrived at the house at around 2.30pm. He treated Sophia for what might be premature labour and then left, believing that he had done all he could to help.

At some time between 4.00pm and 4.30pm, Alfred William Odell, who was Sophia's brother, called to visit her. He heard the story of the argument between Lawrence and Sophia, saw that her condition had not improved and went back to Dr Frankish's surgery at 102 Sloane Street. Dr Frankish was not there, so Odell left a message asking him to call at Lower North Street, as soon as he returned.

Dr Frankish returned to Lower North Street at around 6.15pm. Now, for the first time, he made a thorough examination of his patient and found a wound on her left side, midway between her navel and the edge of her ribs. He treated this wound and left the house again, saying that he would return in a few hours, to check on Sophia's progress.

At 9.30pm, the doctor did return and found that Sophia had, if anything, grown even weaker. Dr Frankish then changed the dressing on Sophia's wound but it was to no avail. At 11.30pm that same night, Sophia Lawrence died in her bed. As for John Thomas Lawrence, who had already been taken into custody, he was now charged with the murder of his wife.

The inquest on the dead woman took place at the *Prince of Wales Tavern* in Exeter Street, Chelsea, on Saturday, 22 February. Here, the jury returned a verdict of manslaughter against Lawrence. However, a later appearance at the Westminster police court, ruled that Lawrence should be charged with murder.

Lawrence's trial for murder took place on 3 March 1890, before the Lord Chief Justice, Lord Coleridge. The case for the Crown was led by Mr Charles Mathews, who was assisted by Mr Horace Avory. Lawrence's defence rested in the hands of Mr Warburton.

John Alfred George Lawrence was the son of the prisoner and he testified that he had been at home on the morning of 20

February and had heard his parents arguing. Even before John left home, at 3.45am, his father was already very drunk. John returned home at 4.00pm to find his mother lying in bed and his father sitting on a chair in the room. He asked his mother what the problem was, but she did not answer him. That evening, at around 8.00pm, John was in the kitchen with his father who suddenly said, quite calmly, 'I threw the knife at mother.'

Alfred Odell told the court that it had been his intention to visit his sister Sophia on 20 February, but his visit was brought forward when he received a message from Mary Ann Morgan, saying that his sister was very ill. Later, at around 5.30pm, Alfred was in the kitchen when Lawrence came in and said, 'Alf, I have done it. I suppose I shall be bloody well hanged for it.'

Detective Samuel Cluny was called to the house at 7.15pm. Having spoken to Dr Frankish, Cluny went to speak to Lawrence who was asleep in an armchair at the time. Cluny woke Lawrence and told him that he would be taken to the police station and charged with stabbing his wife. Lawrence offered no resistance and, when charged at the station, burst into tears. He did the same later that same night, when the charge was changed to one of murder.

In addition to telling of his visits to the house in Lower North Street, and his treatment of Sophia Lawrence, Dr Frankish was able to tell of his findings at the subsequent post-mortem.

Sophia had suffered a single stab wound and the knife had severed a large vein over her intestines and had also wounded the left lobe of her liver. In order to inflict such a wound, a knife would have had to have been thrown with considerable force.

With his own confession to his son and his brother-in-law, there could be no doubt that Lawrence was directly responsible for his wife's death, but the jury accepted that he had not intended to kill her and duly returned a verdict that he was only guilty of manslaughter. Forty-five-year-old Lawrence was then sentenced to ten years in prison.

Chapter 20

Owen Leonard
1891

Robert Mumford had lodged at 22 Swinbrook Road, West Kensington, for some years and knew all the other people who had rooms in the same building. He was used to their comings and goings and also knew that sometimes they argued.

On 30 September 1891, Mumford had retired for the night at 10.00pm and was soon in a deep sleep. However, just over an hour later, at some time after 11.00pm, Mumford was woken from his slumbers, by the noise of quarrelling and scuffling coming from the rooms upstairs.

Mumford knew that those rooms were occupied by Owen Leonard and his partner, Mary Jane Byrne. Even as he rubbed the sleep from his eyes, Mumford heard Mary's voice shouting, 'Don't kill me', followed by the noise of someone running out on to the landing. Still, it was nothing to do with him and Mumford decided that it would be better not to interfere.

Ten minutes after this, Mumford heard screaming coming from the street outside. There was obviously no way he was going to get back to sleep until, at the very least, he went downstairs and told the argumentative couple to keep quiet. However, when he went down into the street he found Mary Byrne lying on the ground outside the house, writhing in pain and moaning. This was obviously a most serious assault, so Mumford went off to find a policeman.

In fact, Robert Mumford found two constables and, returning to Swinbrook Road, one of the officers attended to the injured woman whilst the other went upstairs to arrest Owen Leonard on a charge of assault. As the prisoner was escorted past the scene he was heard to shout to Mary, 'Ain't you dead yet?'

Mary Byrne was taken to St Mary's Hospital where, despite medical treatment, her condition grew steadily worse. On 6 October, her condition was so bad that Leonard was escorted to the hospital, from prison, so that he could be present when Mary's dying deposition was taken. Mary died that same night and the following morning, 7 October, Owen Leonard was charged with manslaughter.

Leonard's trial took place on 16 November, before Mr Justice Hawkins. The first witness was Kate Byrne, the daughter of the dead woman. She confirmed that although they were not married, Owen and Mary had been living together for some twenty-one years. Kate had last seen her mother alive, at St Mary's Hospital, just before she passed away.

After Robert Mumford had given his evidence, Henry Houghton, another lodger at 22 Swinbrook Road, took the stand. He said he had first heard a disturbance at around 11.30pm on 30 September. At one stage he heard Leonard shout, 'Out of the window you go.' This was followed by the sound of a sash-window being opened, and then immediately by a scream. There was then a sickening thud as Mary hit the ground. Henry was unable to say if Leonard had thrown Mary out of the window or if she had jumped in order to escape him.

Sarah Ann Smith lived next door, at 24 Swinbrook Road. She was awake at the time of the argument and was looking out of her bedroom window. She saw the window open at number 22 and Mary coming out of it, feet first. Mary was fully dressed at the time and, once she was outside, she held on to a flower box on the window ledge, for some minutes. Then, perhaps growing tired, or fearful that Leonard was coming for her, Mary let go and fell to the ground. Sarah dashed downstairs to see if she could offer any help and found Mary lying on the ground, bleeding from wounds in her hand and her head.

William Davies was a grocer and operated his business from 48 Swinbrook Road. He too heard the commotion and went down into the street to see what was going on. He found Mary lying near a window sill on the ground floor, moaning loudly and apparently in great pain.

The two police officers, whom Robert Mumford had found, were Constable Jesse Betts and Constable Frederick Hunt. It was Betts who attended to the injured woman and Mary had said to him, 'He struck me on the head with his fist, and I got out of the window of my own accord, to escape his violence.' Betts then left the stricken woman with some of her neighbours whilst he ran for the doctor.

Constable Hunt had gone up to Leonard's rooms, to arrest him. As he entered the room Leonard said, 'Well, I suppose you have come after me.' Hunt replied, 'Yes, I shall charge you with assaulting your wife,' to which Leonard replied, 'Yes, I know I have done wrong, but it is all through jealousy.'

Inspector Francis James Waite was on duty at the Harrow Road police station, when the prisoner was brought in. As details of the charge were being read out by Constable Hunt, Leonard interrupted and said, 'She said she would jump out of the window, but I did not believe her, as she has said it many times before.'

Inspector Waite was also present at the hospital, as Mary made her deposition just before she died. In one part of her statement Mary had said that she told Leonard, 'You shall not have the satisfaction of killing me; I'll do it myself.' It was Waite who later amended the charge against Leonard to one of manslaughter, after Mary had died.

The final witness was Dr Frederick John Orchard Stevenson, of St Mary's Hospital. He had treated Mary and also performed a post-mortem on 7 October. The cause of death had been lockjaw, brought on by the wound she had suffered in her head.

The prosecution argued that Mary had died from lockjaw, a disease that had been caused by one of her wounds. That wound had been caused by a fall from the window and, since Mary had only left her lodgings through that window to escape Leonard's wrath, he was directly responsible for her death. The jury agreed and Leonard was found guilty.

For that offence of manslaughter, Owen Leonard received a sentence of fifteen years in prison.

Chapter 21

John Noble
1892

Eliza Stewart retired to her bed at some time between 9.00pm and 9.30pm on the night of 4 February 1892. By 11.00pm, she was in a deep sleep but a strident knocking at her door at 100 North Street, Chelsea woke her from her slumbers. The caller was the man who lodged in the rooms downstairs, John Noble.

Noble did not mince his words. As a weary-eyed Eliza opened the door he announced, 'Will you come down. Elizabeth is dead.' Then, as if that were not enough, he added, 'I have cut her throat.'

The 'Elizabeth', who Noble was referring to was his partner, forty-year-old Mary Elizabeth Swift, a woman who preferred to use her middle name. Elizabeth had already been married twice; her first husband having died and her second having left her in 1871. She had been living with Noble for the past four or five months.

Eliza Stewart did not have time to go down to see what had happened to Elizabeth Swift, for almost immediately the police, in the form of Constable George Osborn, arrived on the scene. Elizabeth had not actually been attacked in their rooms downstairs, but in the *Friend in Hand* public house. A brother officer had alerted Osborn and he had now gone to number 100, to arrest the man who, witnesses said, had attacked her.

When Constable Osborn arrested Noble he asked if Elizabeth were dead. Told that she was, he replied, 'Poor dear. This is all through jealousy. It has been going on for some time.' Later that same night, Noble was formally charged with murder.

Just over one month later, on 7 March, John Noble appeared in court to answer that charge. Mr Charles Matthews and Mr

Horace Avory acted for the Crown, whilst Noble was defended by Mr Thompson and Mr Bond.

Emma Smith testified that the dead woman was her sister. Having confirmed something of Elizabeth's past life, Emma stated that she had last seen her sister alive at 2.00pm on the day she had been attacked. At the time, Elizabeth was sober and in good health.

Eliza Mills was a shopkeeper, who traded from premises at 89 North Street but she was also a close friend of the dead woman. She testified that at some time between 5.30pm and 5.45pm, Elizabeth had called at her home, to be followed some ten minutes later by the prisoner. At 7.00pm, Eliza, John, Elizabeth and another friend, went to the *Hope and Anchor* public house for a drink. Soon afterwards they went to a number of other establishments, ending up at the *Cranley Arms*.

It was at that latter house that the barman called out, 'Is there anyone of the name Noble here?' John Noble had identified himself and the barman then told him that there was a lady in the next room, who wished to speak to him. Noble then spoke to someone over a partition that separated the two rooms, whereupon Elizabeth Swift shouted, 'That is another of your beautiful women I suppose.'

Despite the obvious atmosphere that now existed between Elizabeth and Noble, the group all moved on to the *Enterprise*, but after one drink, Noble left them there and the group only met up with him again, some time later, in Beauchamp Place. Eliza Mills finally left Noble and Elizabeth at the corner of North Street, assumed they were on their way home, and bade them good night.

Lilly Warner was another resident of 100 North Street and she heard someone coming into the house at around 10.45pm on the fateful night. Though she could not say with certainty who it was, the person did go into the rooms occupied by Noble and Elizabeth and very soon afterwards, Lilly heard Noble say, 'You shan't go out of this house tonight.' A scuffle followed, and the front door then slammed shut. Finally, Lilly heard a scream and upon going outside, saw a group of people around the *Friend in Hand*. Going to investigate, Lilly saw Elizabeth's body lying on the ground nearby.

Philip Mills lived in Marlborough Road, but at around 11.00pm on 4 February, he was walking down North Street, when he saw a woman rush out of number 100. She ran to him, caught hold of his arm and tried to speak to Philip but a gaping wound in her throat meant that she could not speak. Almost immediately, Noble followed her out of the house and shouted, 'Now you can bleed.' Elizabeth then ran off into the *Friend in Hand* and fell on the floor, near the entrance.

Robert Cribble was the barman at the *Friend in Hand* and he told the court that Elizabeth had run into the bar, bleeding badly from the throat. She ran up to the counter and tried to say something but was unable to form any words. Moments later, Noble appeared in the doorway and seeing him there, Elizabeth tried to push past him. Noble reacted by striking her in the side of the head and she fell to the floor in the doorway.

That blow was also seen by John Cutler, who was in the bar at the time. Seeing that Elizabeth was in dire need of assistance, it was Cutler who ran for the doctor.

The first police officer on the scene was Constable Horace Alcock. He had heard someone shout 'Police!' and dashed to the scene. It was Alcock who tried to staunch the bleeding before the doctor arrived.

Doctor Charles Ashley Scott Leggatt found Elizabeth lying on the floor in the bar of the *Friend in Hand*; she had been carried inside by some of the witnesses to the affair. The unfortunate woman died within two minutes of Dr Leggatt's arrival. Having later performed the post-mortem, Dr Leggatt was able to describe a wound some five inches in length and down to the vertebrae of the spine. The wound would have required great force to inflict.

With so much evidence against him, the jury could only really reach one verdict. Finding Noble guilty of murder, they did, however, add a strong recommendation to mercy on account of the provocation they believed he had suffered from Elizabeth.

It did nothing to save Noble's life and he was hanged at Newgate on 29 March, less than two months after he had taken Mary Elizabeth Swift's life.

Chapter 22

Walter Hosler
1892

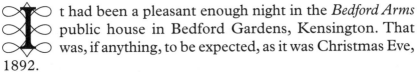

I t had been a pleasant enough night in the *Bedford Arms* public house in Bedford Gardens, Kensington. That was, if anything, to be expected, as it was Christmas Eve, 1892.

At some time between 6.00pm and 7.00pm, the landlord, William Thomas Tilbury, saw one of his regular customers, Walter Hosler, enter the public bar and order himself a pint of beer. Sometime after this, another regular, Dennis Finnessey, entered the same bar. Hosler, noticing Finnessey shouted, 'Here is my old enemy', to which Finnessey replied, 'Yes, that is quite right.'

William Tilbury kept an eye on the two men, in case the discussion escalated and he might have to intervene in order to keep the peace. Fortunately, although there did seem to be a good deal of animosity between the two, the harsh words did not become a physical fight. However, after some time, Tilbury did hear the two men agree to meet on Boxing Day, so that they could fight. Soon afterwards, Hosler left the bar to be followed, within a minute, by Finnessey.

No more than ten minutes passed before a man rushed in and shouted that someone had been stabbed outside. Tilbury dashed into the street to find Finnessey standing in front of the pub window, bleeding profusely from a wound in his neck. There was no sign of Walter Hosler.

Rushed to St Mary's Hospital, Dennis Finnessey was treated for a stab wound to his throat. It was all to no avail and he died later that same night. Hosler, who had been taken into custody on a charge of assault, was now charged with wilful murder.

Walter Hosler appeared at the Old Bailey on 15 January 1893, before Mr Justice Grantham. For the defence, Mr Drake admitted that his client was responsible for Finnessey's death, but claimed that since he had acted in self-defence, the charge should be reduced to manslaughter. That, of course, was for the jury to decide.

Edward Kitt told the court that at some time between 9.30pm and 10.00pm on 24 December, he had been walking along the end of Bedford Gardens and was about to turn into Silver Street, when he saw one man outside the public house and a second standing just around the corner. The man, who he now knew to be Finnessey, was in Silver Street, whilst Hosler was in Bedford Gardens.

Kitt heard Hosler call for Finnessey by name and, as he turned, Hosler appeared to hit him in the neck. A brief struggle followed before Finnessey staggered back against the Bedford Arms, whilst Hosler dashed off up Silver Street. Kitt wasted no time in finding a constable.

David Bryan was inside the *Bedford Arms* and left a few minutes after Finnessey and Hosler. He found Finnessey outside, holding his hand to his neck and leaning against a window. As the blood spurted from between his fingers, Finnessey was able to say that Hosler had attacked him and gone off up Silver Street. Bryan looked down the street and saw Hosler, who was by now walking, in Silver Street and ran after him. Catching him up, Bryan had said, 'Walter, you have stabbed a man; come back with me.' A brief struggle followed, but Hosler was soon subdued and Bryan then escorted him back.

Jonathan Skipmore was another of the customers inside the public house and, after hearing the commotion outside, had gone to see what was happening. He too saw Finnessey, bleeding from a wound in the left side of his neck. By now he was very faint and hardly able to stand.

Constable Thomas Moriarty had been told, by Edward Kitt, that a man had been stabbed outside the *Bedford Arms*. He went to the scene with a brother officer, Constable George Taylor. They saw Finnessey, in a state of collapse, still bleeding badly and it was Taylor who escorted him to the hospital. At the time, Hosler was being held between David Bryan and the landlord, William Tilbury, who handed over a knife, which he had confiscated from Hosler. As the officer spoke to him, Hosler remarked, 'It is my knife. I told him if he hit me again, I would stick him. This is the third time he has set on me.'

Dr Atwood Thorn was the doctor on duty at St Mary's Hospital, when Finnessey was brought in at some time before 10.00pm. There was a very deep, penetrating wound on the left side of Finnessey's neck. The wound was at least three inches deep and had severed some of the major veins in the neck. Despite treatment, Finnessey died eighty minutes later, from loss of blood.

Hosler had, by now, changed his story. It was true that there was bad blood between him and Finnessey and there had been for some time. It was also true that they had had harsh words inside the *Bedford Arms* and had agreed to a fist fight on 26 December. Now, however, despite his earlier statement and confession, Hosler claimed that he had not stabbed Finnessey at all. It must have been another man who then ran off and he had been seized for no other reason than he was in Silver Street, close by the scene of the attack.

The jury chose to believe the earlier confession and the testimony of the various witnesses. Hosler was found guilty and sentenced to death by the judge.

Walter Hosler never did keep his appointment with the hangman. The authorities decided that there had been a good deal of provocation from Finnessey and, as a result, the sentence was commuted to one of imprisonment.

Chapter 23

Reginald Treherne Bassett Saunderson

1895

At 11.30pm, on Sunday, 25 November 1894, Arthur Salter was walking towards 8 Holland Park Road, to collect his daughter. She had been visiting friends, and he planned to escort her home. As Arthur walked along Holland Park Terrace, he saw a young woman lying on the ground, close to some iron railings. Thinking that she was a woman of the lower classes, obviously the worse for drink, Arthur tutted and began to walk on. Only then did he notice that the woman lay in a pool of blood.

Arthur ran on to his destination, rang the doorbell, and told the occupants what he had seen. At the time another gentleman, an artist named Alfred Chautrey Corbould, was also visiting the house. He went out to see the woman for himself and then, realising that Arthur Salter had been telling the truth, went to find a policeman.

In fact, two police officers were soon on the scene. Constable Thomas Gordon and Constable William Patterson arrived at Holland Park Terrace together and, whilst Gordon went to fetch a doctor, Patterson made a careful search of the immediate area. It wasn't long before he found a walking stick in a gutter nearby.

In a modern-day investigation, the scene of the attack would be cordoned off and remain undisturbed. At this time, though, procedures were rather less formal, so the two officers lifted the body and carried the woman to the police station. There she was seen, at 12.15am on 26 November, by Dr Meredith Townsend, who pronounced 'life extinct'. He estimated that the woman had been dead for approximately half an hour, since her body was still warm and, though a post-mortem would need to be carried out, it was clear that she had been stabbed in the stomach and had probably bled to death.

The woman carried no form of identification, so a list of her belongings was made. She wore a black skirt, a red-striped flannelette bodice, low shoes and a black hat, trimmed with white lace. She also wore two rings on the third finger of her left hand, perhaps indicating that she was a married woman. A description of the woman and her clothing was published and this led Lilian Creber to come forward and make a positive identification. The victim of the attack was a thirty-year-old prostitute named Augusta Dawes.

The inquest on the dead woman opened on 29 November, at Kensington Town Hall, before the coroner, Mr C Luxmore Drew. Details of the formal identification by Lilian Creber were given and it was confirmed that she was also a prostitute and had lived with Augusta at 36 St Clement's Road. She had last seen Augusta at 8.00pm on 25 November, when she left home, saying that she was going to Kensington.

Another witness was Kate Forsyth, who had once lodged with Augusta. She confirmed that the dead woman had never been married, but had had two children, one of whom was now living in the workhouse.

One other curious piece of information was given at the inquest. A letter had been handed over to the police. It bore a Belfast postmark and, dated 28 November, it was a full confession to the crime. The letter was signed Jack the Ripper. It must be remembered that the horrific Whitechapel crimes had only taken place in London some six years earlier and there was, initially, a good deal of press speculation that Jack had returned to the streets. This was, however, quickly dispelled and soon those same newspapers were confirming that this was not a crime of the Ripper type.

Over the next few days, more details of Augusta Dawes' life were revealed. She had been a native of Bristol, but had left there, for London, some five years before. At the time she had been a most respectable lady, but she soon fell in with two gentlemen who were business partners. Apparently, both of these men were attracted to Augusta and both made advances towards her. Augusta chose to take one as a lover and rejected the other, leading to animosity between the two partners. They argued and an assault took place, which ended with one of the partners being sent to prison. Not long after this, Augusta had found herself pregnant, whereupon her lover abandoned her

Soon after this, Augusta found herself another lover and they began living together in 1892. Unfortunately, her bad luck had not improved and very soon afterwards, this new man was sentenced to ten years in prison for fraud. Augusta turned to drink and was forced to seek a living by selling her body on the streets.

In fact, although there were no such reports in the newspapers of the day, the police net was already closing in on the man who had attacked and killed Augusta Dawes. The dead woman's landlady had told the police that Augusta had told her that she had recently met two men, one of whom she described as tall and dark who carried a cherry walking stick. That description matched the stick found at the scene, which indicated that the police were looking for a tall, dark man.

Next, there was the fact that a report had come in that a man, fitting that description, had recently absconded from a mental institution, not far from London. That man was also tall and dark. Then, there was the mysterious confession signed 'Jack the Ripper'. That had been posted from Ireland to a friend of the wanted man and, when the handwriting on that letter was compared to known samples of the mental patient, a positive match was found. The police now knew that they were looking for twenty-one-year-old Reginald Saunderson.

Saunderson came from a most distinguished family, his father being Colonel Saunderson, the Member of Parliament for North Armagh. Contact with the family led to the wanted man's location and Saunderson had been found. A warrant for his arrest was drawn up on 4 December, and executed in Armagh, the following day. Plans for his removal to London were immediately put into place.

By now, another important witness had come forward. Herbert Schmalz had been going to post a letter, at some time before 11.30pm on 25 November. As he strolled towards the post box in Holland Park Terrace, he saw a young couple walking some yards in front of him. Suddenly, the man threw one arm around the woman's shoulders and appeared to strike her in the stomach. Schmalz did not see the knife and thought this had been just a severe blow to the stomach. He shouted out, 'What are you doing you brute?' The man turned, and seeing Schmalz running towards him, ran off. Schmalz had given chase but lost the man near Warwick Gardens. When the police then searched in that area, they found a bloodstained knife embedded in some timber in a builder's yard, some 100 yards from the scene of the attack. Unfortunately for Augusta, Schmalz did not return to the scene of the crime. If he had, then perhaps Augusta's life may have been saved.

Transferred back to England, Saunderson made a brief appearance at the West London Police Court on 10 December, where it was revealed that he had been in a mental institution at Hampton Wick, for six years. He had walked out of there on the afternoon of 25 November, but his disappearance had not been noticed until 8.30pm. After Augusta had been killed, Saunderson borrowed some money from a teacher at a school he had once attended, and used it to travel to Belfast. From there he had written a letter to a friend, in which he confessed to the murder, signing it Jack the Ripper.

The court returned a verdict that Augusta Dawes had been murdered by Reginald Saunderson and he was committed for trial at the next sessions. The trial actually took place on 28 January 1895, before Mr Justice Wills and it was clear from the outset that the state of Saunderson's mind would be a major factor in the proceedings.

Before any evidence could possibly be heard, the court had to decide if Saunderson was fit to plead to the charge of murder. Dr George Walker, the surgeon at Holloway prison, where Saunderson had been held on remand, said that he was certainly insane and was unfit to plead to the indictment against him. Dr

Walker went on to say that Saunderson's mental condition had deteriorated even further whilst he had been in custody and he had become so violent at times that he had been placed in a straightjacket inside a padded cell. This evidence was confirmed by Dr Edgar Shepherd, who had also made careful observations of the prisoner inside Holloway.

The prosecution offered no arguments against the medical evidence and, after some discussion, the judge ruled that Saunderson was insane and had been at the time he took Augusta's life. There was only one sentence possible and Saunderson was then informed that he would be detained until Her Majesty's pleasure be known.

Chapter 24

Alice Jane Money
1908

lizabeth Maud Baines lived at 75 Onslow Dwellings, in Pond Place, Chelsea, with her husband and children. Living at the same address was Maud's lodger, Alice Money, and her husband, Joseph. The Moneys also had two children, four-year-old Daisy and Norah, who was one year and nine months old.

At 11.40am on Tuesday, 28 January 1908, Elizabeth Baines was at her window, singing to her children, when Alice Money passed by. Alice remarked, 'You are singing. Have you done all your work?' The two women chatted together for a short time until Alice said that she had a very bad headache. Elizabeth said she had some Seidlitz powders in the house and asked Alice if she would like one. Alice replied, 'No, I am going to get a powder for my head, and I will take the baby with me.'

Elizabeth did not see Alice again until 4.20pm when she saw her standing at the front door, apparently in some sort of daze. Elizabeth asked her lodger if she was feeling all right and Alice said, 'My head is still so bad.' Then, before Elizabeth could continue the conversation, Alice added, 'I must tell you, my baby is dead.' Elizabeth thought she must have misheard and asked, 'Dead?' To this Alice replied, 'Yes, I have cut its throat.'

Not sure as to what she should do now, Elizabeth took Alice inside the house and sat her down upon a chair. She then called for her husband, Joseph, told him what Alice had said, and asked him to go for the police. Even as Elizabeth was telling her husband the story, Alice again said that she had cut her baby's throat, adding that she had also cut her own and taken something from a bottle.

It was around 5.00pm when Constable Richard Jones arrived

at the house. He noticed that Alice Money had a scarf tied quite tightly around her neck and, on a hunch, he stepped forward and loosened it. Beneath the scarf, Alice had inflicted a slight wound upon her own throat and there was some blood. Constable Jones told Joseph Baines to go for a doctor.

Meanwhile, Constable Jones went into Alice's bedroom where he found Norah Money lying on the bed, her face covered with a shawl. On removing the shawl, Jones saw that the child's throat had been cut through deeply. It was clear that the child was beyond all aid and Jones then returned to Alice and cautioned her. She replied, 'I did it at about half past twelve.' Later that same day, Alice was charged with the murder of her infant daughter.

Alice Money appeared at the Old Bailey, before Mr Justice Bucknill, on 3 March 1908. Mr AE Gill and Mr Leycester appeared for the prosecution and Alice was defended by Mr AW Elkin, who entered a plea that his client had been insane at the time she committed the crime.

Dr James Hamilton said that he had been called to Onslow Dwellings, where he had found a superficial throat wound on the prisoner. That wound was almost certainly self-inflicted. He later examined the body of Norah Money and confirmed that life was extinct. She had been dead for some hours and the pillows and bedclothes were saturated with blood.

The divisional police surgeon, Dr James Robert Hayes, had also been called to the scene of the crime. He stated that Alice appeared to be in some sort of daze and did not realise what she had done. Later he did the post-mortem on Norah and confirmed that in life she had been a well-nourished child. Dr Hayes had also been handed a bottle, found inside Alice's rooms. He confirmed that it had contained oxalic acid but, having examined Alice's mouth, he doubted that she had actually taken any.

Inspector Alfred Ward had also gone to the house on the day of Norah's death. He testified that the rooms were exceptionally clean and tidy. Alice had obviously taken good care of the house and, by all accounts, was a good mother and wife.

How the *Illustrated Police News* showed the finding of one of the victims of Walter Miller. Author's Collection

The finding of the body of Augusta Dawes in Holland Park Terrace. A sketch from the *Illustrated Police News*. Author's Collection

The Imperial Institute where Madan Lal Dhingra shot two men dead. Author's Collection

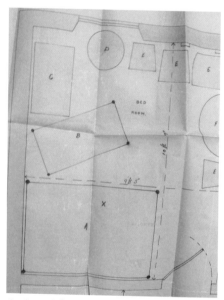

A plan of the room where Alice Jane Money claimed the life of her child, Norah. The National Archives

Madan Lal Dhingra. Author's Collection

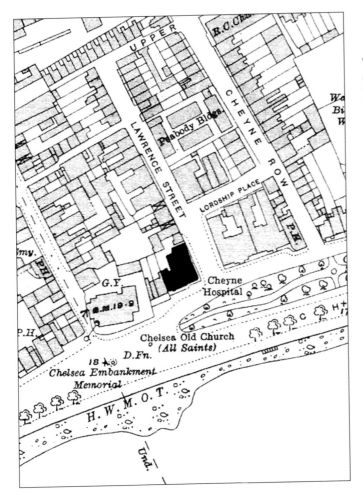

The location of the *Cross Keys* public house where Frances Buxton was murdered.
Alan Godfrey Maps

The document detailing the commuting of the death sentence on Ronald True.
The National Archives

Sir,

I am directed by the Secretary of State to acquaint you that he has had under his consideration the case of Ronald True, now in the Prison at Pentonville, having been sentenced to death, and that he has advised His Majesty to respite the capital sentence with a view to the immediate removal of the convict to Broadmoor Criminal Lunatic Asylum. The convict has been certified to be insane under section 2(4) of the Criminal Lunatics Act, 1884.

I am,

Sir,

Your obedient Servant

E. Blackwell

The Commissioner of Police

It was on these steps that O'Sullivan and Dunne shot dead their victim, Field Marshal Sir Henry Wilson. Author's Collection

Sir Henry Wilson,
the murdered man.
Author's Collection

The key to the storeroom. It was used as an exhibit at Harvey's trial. The National Archives

The storeroom where George Frank Harvey killed George Hamblin. The National Archives

The body of George Hamblin, in situ. The National Archives

One of the many letters Harold Dorian Trevor wrote to the authorities whilst he was in custody. The National Archives

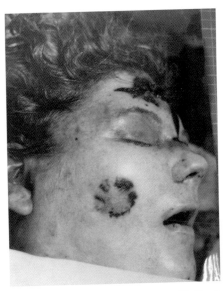

A close up of the facial injuries Winifred suffered. The round-shaped wound was inflicted by a hammer.
There was an identical mark on her other cheek. The National Archives

Number 17 Finborough Road, where George Epton killed Winifred Mulholland. He lived in the flat with the balcony. The National Archives

The body of Winifred Mulholland. The National Archives

Winifred Mulholland
in life. The National
Archives

The killer, George Cyril Epton. The National Archives

Thomas John Ley. Author's Collection

John George Haigh.
Author's Collection

Haigh's final victim, Mrs
Olive Durand-Deacon.
Author's Collection

The police search of the yard at Crawley. Author's Collection

The public queuing outside Lewes courthouse for the trial of John George Haigh. Author's Collection

Christine Granville.
Author's Collection

The killer, Dennis George
Muldowney. Author's Collection

Part of the report on Muldowney's execution. The National Archives

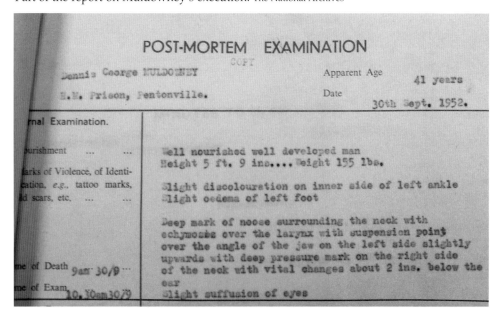

POST-MORTEM EXAMINATION
COPY

Dennis George MULDOWNEY

H.M. Prison, Pentonville.

Apparent Age
41 years

Date
30th Sept. 1952.

...rnal Examination.

...urishment ... ...

...arks of Violence, of Identi-
...cation, e.g., tattoo marks,
...d scars, etc. ... ...

Well nourished well developed man
Height 5 ft. 9 ins..... Weight 155 lbs.

Slight discolouration on inner side of left ankle
Slight oedema of left foot

Deep mark of noose surrounding the neck with
echymosis over the larynx with suspension point
over the angle of the jaw on the left side slightly
upwards with deep pressure mark on the right side

...me of Death 9am 30/9 ...

...me of Exam 10.10am 30/9

of the neck with vital changes about 2 ins. below the
ear
Slight suffusion of eyes

Christine Granville's body in the foyer of the *Shelborne Hotel*. The National Archives

A police picture of Christine's body. Note the murder weapon lying off to the left. The National Archives

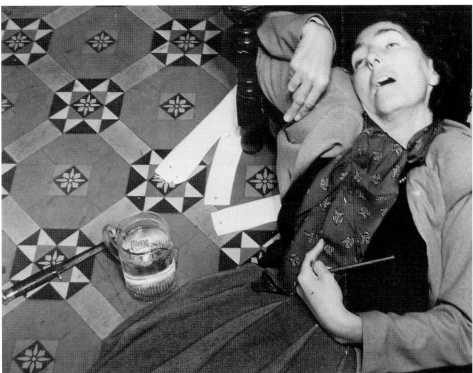

The reception area of the *Aban Court Hotel.*
The National Archives

The body of George Smart, as it was discovered. The National Archives

A close-up of George Smart's body, once it had been turned over by the doctor, for examination. The National Archives

The flat at 17 Walpole Street where Robert Lipman killed Claudie Delbarre. Her rooms were on the top floor. The National Archives

The body of Claudie Delbarre, in her bed. The National Archives

Robert Lipman, the killer from New York. The National Archives

Only two witnesses were called for the defence. Joseph Money told the court that he and Alice had been married for about five years. They had been happy enough, until the last three months or so, when Alice had started complaining of severe head pains. Ever since she had behaved irrationally and had suffered from mood swings and fits of temper. Often she had not been aware of what she had done until the headache passed.

Joseph also told the court that he and his wife had argued the night before Norah's death. Apparently, Alice had taken to pawning items of late, even though they did not need the money. He had discovered that she had just pawned her wedding ring and this had upset him greatly. They had had words and that night he had slept on the couch in the living room. Alice had come in, at around 10.00pm, and asked him to come to bed but he had refused. Alice had then covered him with some coats, in case he got cold during the night.

Dr Fullerton was the deputy medical officer at Holloway prison and had observed Alice since her incarceration. He found her to be suffering from very deep depression and during her time in the cells, had often complained of terrible headaches. He had no doubt that she was insane at the time she took her daughter's life.

Those final two witnesses swayed the jury who found Alice guilty of murder but insane. Having avoided a death sentence, Alice was then sentenced to be detained until a further order was made by the appropriate authorities.

Chapter 25

Madan Lal Dhingra
1909

The entertainment in the Jehangir Hall in the Imperial Institute, South Kensington, on Thursday, 1 July 1909, had been enjoyed by all of the distinguished guests and now, as the meeting broke up, people gathered in small groups to talk and discuss the speeches that they had heard. One of the guests, Sir William Hutt Curzon-Wylie, the Aide-de-Camp to the Secretary of State for India, stood in the doorway, talking to some people.

One of the people Sir William was speaking to was a young Indian gentleman, wearing evening dress and a blue turban. Suddenly, as people still milled about, the young Indian raised his hand and pointed a gun directly at Sir William's head. Four shots were fired directly into Sir William's head. These shots were followed by a pause, and then another shot rang out. For some moments, all the other guests in the room were shocked into inactivity but, after the fifth shot was fired, a number of men moved forward to grab the assailant. One of those men was Dr Cowas Lalcaca and as he approached, the young Indian raised the gun once more and fired a bullet into Dr Lalcaca's stomach. Finally, the young Indian raised the gun to his own temple and pulled the trigger. There was a loud click. The assailant was out of ammunition. He was immediately seized and pinned to the floor, pending the arrival of the police.

The first police officer on the scene was Constable Frederick Nicholls. By now, the man who had fired those six shots was on his feet and being held by several men. He offered no resistance, as Nicholls took him into custody, or as the officer searched him. Within a few minutes, Detective Sergeant Frank Eadley arrived at the Institute and he assisted Nicholls to escort the prisoner to

Marylebone police station. There, the young man identified himself as Madan Lal Dhingra, a student. Lal Dhingra had been born in the Punjab on 18 February 1883 to a family, who were loyal to the British. As a young man he had studied at Lahore, but had been expelled due to his political activities. He had then travelled to England, arriving here in 1906 and enrolling as a student of mechanical engineering at University College.

At the police station, Lal Dhingra was informed that both Sir William and Dr Lalcaca were dead, and in the early hours of 2 July, he was charged with murdering both men. He made a full written statement, explaining his motives for the crimes.

Later that same day, Friday, 2 July, Madan Lal Dhingra appeared at the Westminster Police Court. The evidence having been heard, the prisoner was duly sent for trial on the capital charge. His trial took place exactly three weeks later, on 23 July, before the Lord Chief Justice, Lord Alverstone. A formidable array of legal talent lined up for the prosecution. Led by the Attorney General, Sir William Robson, he was assisted by Mr Bodkin, Mr Rowlatt and Mr Leycester. Lal Dhingra had no legal representation whatsoever.

At the start of the trial, Lal Dhingra refused to be represented, saying that he did not recognise the court. In his opinion, as far as Sir William was concerned, he had committed no crime. He had merely assassinated an enemy of his country. As for the death of Dr Lalcaca, that had been nothing more than a tragic accident and was a case of self-defence. Despite his remonstrations, a formal not guilty plea was entered and evidence called on just the one offence; the murder of Sir William.

Mrs Harris lived at 106 Ledbury Road, Bayswater, and she testified that the prisoner had come to lodge with her on Easter Monday, 1909. On the day of the shooting, 1 July, he had left her house at 2.00pm. He had returned at around 8.00pm in order to change for a meeting he said he was going to. He had changed quickly and left soon afterwards.

William Burrow was an assistant at Gamage's Store in Holborn. He told the court that his employer sold guns, amongst many other items, and kept a register of purchases. This register confirmed that on 26 January, he had sold a Colt automatic pistol to Madan Lal Dhingra, for the sum of £3 5s.

The next witness proved that Lal Dhingra had then started to practise using that weapon. Henry Stanton Morley owned a shooting range at 92 Tottenham Court Road and he stated that some time around March, Lal Dhingra had started attending the range two or three times a week. Over the next three months he became a much better shot and by now was quite proficient. He always brought his own weapon, a Colt automatic, and had last attended on 1 July, at around 5.30pm. Morley then produced the target Lal Dhingra had used on that day. He had fired twelve shots at a target 18 feet away, and scored eleven hits.

Miss Beck was the Honorary Secretary of the National Indian Association, the group who had organised the events of 1 July at the Institute. She began by confirming that Sir William had been a member of the Council and the Honorary Treasurer of the group.

Miss Beck went on to say that she had first encountered Lal Dhingra in March 1909, when he had written to say that he was interested in attending meetings or talks given by the Association. There had been a talk given in May and she had sent him an invitation, but he did not attend. The next time she had contacted Lal Dhingra was to send him an invitation for the discussion on the evening of 1 July. She had seen him there, at around 10.30pm, and spoke to him briefly. She knew that he was a student at University College and asked him about his course. He explained that he had now completed his studies and was about to return to India.

Douglas William Thorburn was a journalist and he was at the Institute to cover the meeting for his newspaper. At 11.00pm, he was in the main hall when he happened to glance up. He saw Lal Dhingra, apparently in conversation with Sir William, in the doorway. He saw the prisoner raise a gun and fire four shots directly into Sir William's face. Moments later, he saw Dr Lalcaca fall to the floor after being shot. Thorburn was one of the men who then ran forward and helped push Lal Dhingra to the floor.

Sir Leslie Probyn was another of the guests at the meeting. He too saw the shots being fired and went to help Thorburn and others pin the shooter to the ground. It was Probyn who wrestled the gun from Lal Dhingra's hand and later handed it over to the police.

Captain Charles Rolleston had his back to the shooting, but turned in time to see Lal Dhingra fire at an Indian gentleman in evening dress. He now knew that gentleman to be Dr Lalcaca and Rolleston saw him fall backwards, after he had been shot.

After Constable Nicholls and Sergeant Eadley had given their testimony, Inspector Albert Draper took the stand. He had had charge of Lal Dhingra at the police court and he testified that after the proceedings had closed, Lal Dhingra spoke to him saying; 'The only thing I want to say is that there was no wilful murder in the case of Dr Lalcaca. I did not know him and when he advanced to take hold of me, I simply fired in self-defence.'

Doctor Thomas Neville had been called to the Institute to examine both victims of the attack. Later, at the police station, he examined the prisoner and found him to be calm, collected and quiet. Dr Neville checked Lal Dhingra's pulse and found it to be perfectly regular and normal.

Neville had performed both post-mortems, but only detailed the wounds suffered by Sir William. He had been shot in the right eye and there was a corresponding exit wound at the back of his neck. There were two wounds just over his left eye and another below his left ear. Death would have been instantaneous.

After all the evidence had been heard, Lal Dhingra was asked if he had anything to say in his own defence. He replied, 'I have nothing to say. I admit that I did it. The evidence is all true. I should like my statement read.'

The statement Lal Dhingra referred to was a long one he had made after his arrest. This was then read out in court. It began: 'I do not want to say anything in defence of myself, but simply to prove the justice of my deed. As for myself, no English law court has got any authority to arrest and detain me in prison, or pass sentence of death on me.'

The statement continued: 'And I maintain that if it is patriotic in an Englishman to fight against the Germans, if they were to occupy this country, then it is much more justifiable and patriotic in my case to fight against the English.

'I hold the English people responsible for the murder of eighty millions of Indian people in the last fifty years, and they are also responsible for taking £100,000,000 every year from India to this country.

'I also hold then responsible for the hanging and deportation of my patriotic countrymen, who did just the same as the English people here are advising their countrymen to do.

'Just as the Germans have no right to occupy this country, so the English people have no right to occupy India, and it is perfectly justifiable on our part, to kill the Englishman who is polluting our sacred land.

'I make this statement, not because I wish to plead for mercy or anything of that kind. I wish that English people should sentence me to death, for in that case the vengeance of my countrymen will be all the more keen. I put forward this statement, to show the justice of my cause to the outside world, and especially to our sympathisers in America and Germany.'

The verdict was a formality, the jury not even bothering to leave the court before returning it, and Lal Dhingra was then sentenced to death. He listened in silence as the death sentence was intoned and then replied, 'Thank you my Lord. I don't care. I am proud to have the honour of laying down my life for the cause of my motherland.'

There was no appeal and no reprieve. On Tuesday, 17 August, twenty-six-year-old Madan Lal Dhingra was hanged at Pentonville prison by Henry Pierrepoint and his brother, Thomas.

The authorities had refused one of Lal Dhingra's last requests: that his body be granted Hindu burial rites, and he was interred in a grave within the prison. There he remained until December 1976 when his body was exhumed, along with that of Udham Singh, another Indian hanged in 1940 for a political assassination.

Both bodies were then repatriated to India.

Chapter 26

The Murder of Frances Buxton
1920

It was a matter of routine for the constable on the beat around Lawrence Street, Chelsea. He would patrol the area, trying the doors of the various business premises, in order to make sure that all was secure. Things were no different on the morning of Sunday, 18 January 1920.

The officer came to the *Cross Keys* public house, a curiously isolated building, within the borough of Chelsea. The pub stood alone with a passageway at each side. One of those passageways led to a piece of wasteland, which led to the back of All Saints' Church. The other separated the *Cross Keys* from a fairly new block of flats. With such a position to consider, the officer thought that it would be better to check the back door of the pub, as well as the front. The front door was securely locked but, when he tried the rear door, the constable found, to his surprise, that it was open.

The police officer entered the pub, calling out if anyone was there. Then, suddenly, he noticed the smell of burning and it seemed to be coming from the direction of the cellar. Going to investigate further, the constable found smoke issuing from a pile of what appeared to be sacks and sawdust in the cellar. He immediately called in the fire brigade.

It didn't take long for the brigade to douse down the sacking but, when it was removed, they found a woman's body underneath the sawdust. Further investigation showed that the woman had been battered about the head, by some sort of blunt instrument. Dried blood and sawdust were caked about the woman's head and it was clear that this was no tragic accident. The police were looking at a case of murder and the victim was the landlady of the premises, fifty-five-year-old Frances Buxton.

The inquest on the dead woman opened on Tuesday, 20 January. Frank Charles Buxton, the owner of the *Sussex Hotel*, near Bexhill, testified that he was Frances's husband, but added that they had not lived together for eleven or twelve years. He had asked her, on more than one occasion, to give up the *Cross Keys*, or at least to stop living on her own, but she had been a most strong willed woman and made up her own mind.

Evidence was given that when Frances's body had been found, the upper portion of it was buried in sawdust. In addition to the sacking thrown over the body, there was also more stuffed beneath her legs. The wounds on the head were extreme and the weapon used to inflict them was, almost certainly, a bottle. Pieces of glass had been found scattered about the body, which had been lying in a pool of blood, and a broken bottle had been found in a passageway close by.

Elizabeth Mitchell was a barmaid at the *Cross Keys* and she had left the premises at her usual time, after the bar had closed, on the night of Saturday, 17 January. At the time, there would have been around £20 in the till, being that day's takings. Elizabeth was also able to say that, during the time she served in the bar, Frances was in the habit of wearing quite a lot of jewellery and some of this now seemed to be missing.

Continuing her testimony, Elizabeth stated that, after the bar closed each night, it was Frances's routine to go down to the cellar to sort out the barrels and other matters for the next day's business.

Lily Mitchell was Elizabeth's daughter and she also helped out behind the bar. Lily had been there on the Saturday night and she remembered that not long before closing time, a man came in. The pub was empty at the time, which was why Lily noticed him in particular. The man was still there when Lily finished work for the night. Lily was able to furnish at least part of a description. The man was tall and fairly well-dressed with greying hair. Unfortunately, he wore a cloth cap, which he kept pulled well down so that Lily did not get a good look at his face.

Lily was also able to give details of two other possible suspects. Some years before, Frances had taken on a man, as a working partner, at the *Cross Keys*. The partnership had not lasted long and had not been helped by the fact that one day, the man had attacked Frances and held her down. Finally, Lily was able to tell the court of a man she had seen in the bar on the Thursday before Frances died.

The man was simply enjoying a quiet pint but he kept looking up, at Frances. In fun, Lily had said to her employer, 'I see there is someone in the bar trying to give you the glad eye.' Frances, however, seemed to be quite concerned. She told Lily that the man had been in for the last three or four days, had been following her, and that she had seen him standing outside, looking up at the house.

The inquest was then adjourned to Tuesday, 3 February, to allow the police to continue with their enquiries. They had the ex-partner to check out, the tall man who had been in the bar on the night Frances was last seen alive, and the mysterious admirer who may or may not have been the same man. They also had clues to go on. Some banknotes, with bloody fingerprints on them, had been found scattered about the bar and matching prints had been found in the blood spatters on the cellar wall. Unfortunately, those prints did not match any known criminals and the police were unable to trace either the tall man, or the admirer.

When the inquest re-opened, the first witness was Anne O'Connor. She had been a customer of the *Cross Keys* on Saturday, 17 January and she too had seen the tall man. However, she was also unable to give a detailed description, meaning that her evidence did not take the investigation any further forward.

Mrs Harvey was a regular customer at the pub and a good friend of Frances'. On Friday, 16 January, they had been in conversation and Frances remarked that a man had been trying to thrust his companionship on her. Foolishly, she had told him that she lived alone. If anything, this seemed to encourage him and he became even more obsessive. On one occasion, Frances had even had to throw him out of the private parlour of the bar, when he became too forward. Was this man the same tall man, who had been in the bar that fateful night, or perhaps the man who had given her the 'glad eye'?

By now the police had to admit that all avenues of inquiry had been explored and all had come to nothing. They had not been able to trace any of the men referred to and it was highly likely that no arrest would ever be made. Having heard all that evidence, the jury had little choice but to return the expected verdict of, 'wilful murder against some person or persons unknown'.

The murder of Frances Buxton is still listed as unsolved.

Chapter 27

Ronald True
1922

On 17 June 1891, a sixteen-year-old unmarried girl, Annabel True, gave birth to a son, whom she named Angus Ronald. As he grew up, the boy dropped his first name and would, for the rest of his days, be known simply as Ronald True.

In 1902, things improved greatly for Annabel, when she married a wealthy man who then became Ronald's step-father. Determined that something should be made of the somewhat feckless eleven-year-old boy, he determined that Ronald should be sent to Bedford Grammar School. It did nothing to help Ronald, for he was by now a liar, a confirmed truant and displayed signs of cruelty towards animals.

In 1908, at the age of seventeen, Ronald left school and, no doubt, would simply have been content to be idle and living off his step-father's money, but that gentleman was having none of it. Through his influence, a number of jobs were found for Ronald, but he either lost them all, or walked out after a month or so. Thus, Ronald tried sheep farming in New Zealand, where one day he earned himself a criminal record by stealing a bicycle in order to travel to a boxing match that he was taking part in. From there he moved on to Argentina, followed by Canada, where he spent a short time as an officer in the Royal Canadian Mounted Police. From Canada he moved on to Mexico and also spent time in Brazil.

By 1914, Ronald was in San Francisco, earning a precarious living as a prize-fighter, until one day he forged some money orders, for which he was arrested. Claiming that he was the Honourable Arthur Reginald French, also known as Lord De

Freyne of Scotland he was, nevertheless, sentenced to fifteen months in prison, being released early in 1915.

By this time, of course, the Great War was raging in Europe and, somewhat uncharacteristically perhaps, Ronald decided that he would join up and serve his country. He joined the Royal Flying Corps but, yet again, this was not to lead to the making of Ronald True. In February 1916, he crashed his plane on his first solo flight, at Farnborough. Luckily he was not seriously injured, though he did suffer some severe concussion. He was back in the air the following month but then managed to crash again. This second crash was followed by a nervous breakdown and, in October 1916, Ronald True was invalided out of the service.

Still with no real purpose in life, Ronald then moved to New York where, using his talent for lying to its fullest extent, he regaled all who would listen with tales of dog-fights he had had with German pilots on the Western Front. Those tales attracted, amongst others, a young would-be actress named Frances Roberts. She and Ronald started walking out together and they married, honeymooning in Mexico, then travelling on to Cuba and, finally, returning to England.

Ronald's step-father was still determined that something should be done for his rather idle step-son and yet another position was found for him, this time with a mining company in the Gold Coast. Ronald started working there in February 1919 but had managed to lose the job within six months. The family had had enough. Ronald was given a generous allowance and told to fend for himself.

By this time, Ronald True had developed another problem. Soon after his two crashes in 1916, he had started experimenting with morphine and by 1919, he was addicted to the drug. A number of spells inside various nursing homes followed, but it did nothing to wean Ronald from his habit. In fact, this led to another brush with the law when, in September 1921, Ronald was fined by Portsmouth magistrates for using forged prescriptions to satisfy his habit.

Things were growing steadily worse and by this time, so dependent had Ronald become, that his behaviour, always rather erratic, began to deteriorate still further. He began to show hostility and violent behaviour towards his wife and his mental state grew ever worse. Now, whenever anything went wrong in his life, Ronald blamed it on another man named Ronald True who was following him, impersonating him and doing all the bad things he was being blamed for. This second Ronald True was a complete figment of Ronald's imagination, but real enough to Ronald himself.

In early 1922, Ronald disappeared in London. He spent his time living in various hotels and was out every night drinking, dancing and womanising. In February of that year he met up with an out of work motor mechanic named James Armstrong and the two became instant friends. Now Ronald had a companion with whom he spent most days and nights and the two became well known in the watering holes of London's west end. One day, Ronald even bought a gun from Armstrong, to protect himself in case he should bump into the other Ronald True.

On Saturday, 18 February, Ronald met a new woman, an attractive twenty-five-year-old prostitute whose real name was Gertrude Yates, but who worked under the assumed name of Olive Young. They spent that night together at her well-furnished, basement flat at 13a Finborough Road. However, perhaps confusing the normal arrangements in such cases, Ronald did not pay his companion, but instead stole a £5 note from her purse before he left the flat.

On 2 March, Ronald decided that it would be better if he had some transport to take him to his various haunts around the capital. So, on that day, he contacted a hire company and booked a chauffeur-driven car. The gentleman detailed to drive him, and James Armstrong, around London was Luigi Mazzola. The two men would spend the day being driven from bar to bar, finally dismissing the driver late each night.

At the same time, Ronald became rather eager to renew his acquaintance with Gertrude Yates. Completely ignoring the fact that he had stolen money from her, Ronald ordered Mazzola to drive him to Gertrude's flat each night, just before midnight. This visit occurred on three consecutive nights: 2-4 March, but on each of these occasions, Gertrude was out. However, on the night of Sunday, 5 March, Gertrude was home and, for some unknown reason, she let Ronald True back into her flat.

On Monday, 6 March, at around 7.10am, the paperboy delivered the *Daily Mirror* to 13a Finborough Road. Some twenty minutes later, at 7.30am, the milkman delivered a pint of milk. Soon after this, Ronald True used some of that milk to make two cups of tea. He placed one on a bedside cabinet and handed the other to Gertrude Yates who sat up in bed to drink it. Then, without any warning, Ronald took a rolling pin he had picked up from the kitchen and battered Gertrude five times about the head. Satisfied that she was dead, he then dragged or carried her body to the bathroom where he left her.

At 9.15am, Emily Steel, the daily maid, arrived to clean the flat. Emily was fully aware of her employer's occupation, so was not surprised to see a man's coat and scarf in the kitchen. No doubt a client had been invited to stay the night. It was none of Emily's business, so she set about cooking some sausages for Gertrude's breakfast.

As the sausages sizzled in the pan, Ronald True entered the kitchen. Emily recognised him as a man she had seen there before, so was not alarmed in any way. Indeed, the considerate gentleman even remarked, 'Don't wake Miss Young. We were late last night. She's in a deep sleep. I'll send the car round for her at twelve o'clock.' He then picked up his coat and scarf and, with a smile, went out into the street.

At 9.30am, Emily Steel decided to check on her employer. She knocked on the bedroom door and entered the room only to find it in disarray. There was blood everywhere, splashed up on the walls and all over the bedclothes and there seemed to be someone lying in the bed. Tentatively, Emily pulled back the bedclothes only to find that the shape she had seen was formed by two, heavily bloodstained, pillows and the rolling pin. Going to investigate through the rest of the flat, Emily finally found Gertrude's naked body in the bathroom. A towel had been rammed down her throat and a dressing-gown cord tied tightly around her neck.

Ronald True, meanwhile, had telephoned both James

Armstrong and Luigi Mazzola and the three spent the rest of that day driving to various cafés and bars around London. At 8.40pm, Mazzola dropped the two friends off at the Hammersmith Palace of Varieties and was told that he would not be needed again that night. He then drove the car back to his garage, arriving there at 9.45pm, only to find the police waiting for him.

Emily Steel had told the police about the chauffeur-driven car Ronald True had hired. That car was duly traced and Mazzola interviewed as to Ronald's whereabouts. That, in turn, led officers to the Hammersmith Palace where Detective Inspector Burton saw Ronald and Armstrong in a box. Having arrested his quarry, Inspector Burton took him to the police station and interviewed him at length, Ronald claiming that there had been another man at the flat and he must have been the one who committed the crime.

On Tuesday, 7 March, Ronald True was charged with the murder of Gertrude Yates. His circumstances did little to alter his behaviour and one day, held on remand in Brixton prison, he attacked a fellow inmate, who he believed was trying to steal his food.

The trial began on 1 May, before Mister Justice McCardie, and lasted for five days. The defence was one of insanity, but in the event, the jury ruled that he was guilty of murder and sentenced to death. An appeal was heard on 26 May, and dismissed. Ronald was then moved to Pentonville prison to await his execution.

Ronald True did not, however, die in the execution chamber of Pentonville prison. The medical officer of the prison submitted a report stating that he believed Ronald to be insane and the Home Secretary, Mr Shortt, ordered a panel of medical experts to examine the prisoner and determine whether or not he was sane. They all agreed that Ronald was not sane and the sentence was commuted to one of confinement in a secure hospital.

This decision caused a public outcry, because another case at the time seemed to indicate that there was one law for the rich and another for the poor.

On Tuesday, 14 March, Lady Alice White had been found battered to death in her room at the *Spencer Hotel*, in Portman Street. A young pantry-boy at the hotel, eighteen-year-old Henry Julius Jacoby had been arrested, tried, found guilty and sentenced to death. He too had lost an appeal against that sentence but Jacoby had been hanged on Wednesday, 7 June. The public now demanded to know why a poor servant had been hanged for the murder of a titled lady whilst a rich man had, apparently, been let off after killing a common prostitute. The scandal almost cost the Home Secretary his job but the decision stood and Ronald was free of the noose.

Ronald True was moved from Pentonville to Broadmoor where he spent the rest of his life, dying there in 1951, at the age of sixty.

Chapter 28

Joseph O'Sullivan and Reginald Dunne

1922

The early 1920s was a troublesome time for politicians in Britain. Ireland had, for some time, been arguing for independence and, in 1918, a sign of the intense Irish feeling could be seen in the general election results. The vast majority of the Irish seats had been taken by Sinn Fein, who demanded Home Rule for Ireland.

Britain resisted all such overtures and an undeclared war then broke out between the British and Irish nationalists. The troubles dragged on for the best part of three years before a treaty was signed, in 1921, granting Ireland dominion status within the British Empire.

The Treaty provided an Irish Free State and a separate Loyalist area in Northern Ireland but this in turn led to other problems. There were many Catholics in the north who supported Home Rule, and this led to clashes between them and the Protestant loyalists. During this bloody period more than 500 Catholics in Northern Ireland were murdered and, in many cases, the police seemed to do little to bring the killers to justice.

If the British authorities would do little to protect the Catholics in the north, then the government in the new Irish Free State would have to do what it could. The new prime minister of the State, Michael Collins, decided that the best way to protect Catholics would be to send aid and arms to the north. This would have the added advantage of destabilising the Unionist government and, possibly, lead to a true unification of Ireland.

To every action, there is a reaction. The British government was not prepared to sit back and watch the new Irish state arm dissidents in the north. They would have to send their own agents to the north in order to infiltrate nationalist groups and gather information. The only decision now was who could they put in charge of this operation?

Field Marshal Sir Henry Wilson knew Irish politics very well indeed. He had been the Chief of the British Imperial Staff and a member of parliament for North Down. A vociferous opponent of nationalism, he had made many speeches attacking not just the idea of a free Ireland, but also attacking Catholics in general. He had even made speeches and comments attacking Michael Collins himself. By 1921, Sir Henry's name had been placed on an IRA death list.

Thursday, 22 June 1922, was a warm, pleasant day in London. At around noon, fifty-eight-year-old Sir Henry attended a ceremony at Liverpool Street railway station, where he unveiled a war memorial. Sir Henry made a speech and, once the ceremony had finished, climbed into a taxi to take him home to Eaton Place, in Chelsea.

The taxi finally pulled up outside 36 Eaton Place and Sir Henry paid the fare. The cab pulled away and Sir Henry walked to his front door and began fumbling for his keys. Two men then stepped forward, drew revolvers, and began firing at the Field Marshal.

In all, Sir Henry Wilson received several wounds. One bullet struck him in the left forearm. Two more hit him in the right arm, and two more in the right leg. Another two bullets caused injuries to his left shoulder but the fatal wounds pierced Sir Henry's lungs; chest wounds fired from opposite sides of his body.

Having achieved their objective, the two assassins tried to make good their escape. There had, however, been a number of witnesses to the shooting. A group of men were working in the street nearby and a couple of police constables who were on patrol in the area, heard the shots. A chase began and, at that point, the two gunmen saw a passing taxi cab and tried to hail it. The driver of that cab saw the two men and, thinking that they were nothing more than ordinary fares, pulled in to the kerb and opened his rear door. Some of the witness who had been giving chase shouted, 'Stop them!' and the driver, thinking that there might have been a robbery, pulled his door shut and began following the two men along the street.

One of the two gunmen seemed to be moving slower than the other, and the crowd soon caught up with him and held him. His companion, seeing him seized, turned and went back to offer assistance. More shots were fired and, in all, three more men received wounds, though none of them were fatal. Constable Marsh, Constable Sayer and a man named Alexander Clarke were all injured but, eventually, the two men were overpowered and taken into custody.

The men readily identified themselves as twenty-five-year-old James Connelly and twenty-four-year-old John O'Brien; and both admitted that they were members of the IRA and had shot Sir Henry in reprisal for his actions in Northern Ireland. They were then both charged with murder.

It soon transpired that both men had given false names to the police. Connelly was actually Joseph O'Sullivan and his companion, O'Brien, was Reginald Dunne. Both had served in the British Army in the Great War and both men had been wounded in France. Indeed, O'Sullivan had lost his right leg below the knee, at Ypres, thus explaining why he had been slower than the other gunman, during the chase. At the time of their arrests, Dunne was the second in command of the London branch of the IRA and had previously attended St Ignatius's College. Now he was at St Mary's College, where he was training to be a teacher. As for O'Sullivan, he had been working at the Ministry of Labour.

The assassination of Sir Henry led to a massive public outcry. The newspapers of the day bayed for the blood of the two killers. The coalition government came under increasing pressure to stop any policy of compromise with Michael Collins and his Irish Free State and, at one stage, it even looked as if war might break out between Britain and Ireland.

The trial of O'Sullivan and Dunne took place at the Old Bailey on 18 July 1922, before Mr Justice Shearman. O'Sullivan was defended by Mr Artemis Jones whilst Dunne was represented by Mr Jeremiah McVeagh. The prosecution case was led by Sir Ernest Pollock, who was assisted by Mr Eustace Fulton, Mr Travers Humphreys and Mr Giveen. The proceedings would last for just three hours.

The trial opened with the charges being read out and both men were then asked how they wished to plead. Dunne replied, 'I admit shooting Sir Henry Wilson.' That, of course, was not a plea so the Clerk of Arraigns asked, 'Are you guilty or not guilty of the murder?' Dunne replied, 'That is the only statement I can make.' After O'Sullivan had replied to the charge in a similar manner, a formal plea of not guilty was entered and the prosecution then outlined its case.

There could be little doubt that the jury would return guilty verdicts, but at the end of the trial, both men were asked if they had anything to say in their defence. Dunne's defence then handed the judge a written statement, which Dunne wished to be read out in court. The judge read through the document and then said, 'I cannot allow this to be read. It is not a defence to the jury at all. It is a political manifesto. It is a justification of the right to kill.'

Though it was not read out in court at the time, the text of that statement is available in The National Archives, and deserves to be quoted in full. It read:

Lord and Members of the Jury. My friend and I stand here before you today charged with the offence of murder; and I have no doubt that, from the evidence placed before you by the prosecution, you will find us both guilty. With respect to the charges of attempted murder, we merely tried, as everyone must know, to try and escape arrest.

The offence of murder is a very serious matter; so much so, that any act which results in loss of human life requires very grave and substantial reason. We have never until now been charged with any crime. As you have heard from the police officer, who gave evidence as to our character and our previous records, we have both been in the British Army.

We both joined voluntarily, for the purpose of making Europe safe in order that the principles for which this country stood, should be upheld and preserved. These principles, we were told, were self-

determination and freedom for small nations. We both, as I have said, fought for these principles, and were commended for doing so; and I imagine that several of you gentlemen of this jury did likewise.

We came back from France to find that self-determination had been given to some nations we had never heard of, but that it had been denied to Ireland. We found, on the contrary that our country was being divided into two countries; that a Government had been set up for the Belfast district, and that under that Government outrages were being perpetrated, that are a disgrace to civilization.

Many of the outrages are being committed by men in uniform and in the pay of the Belfast Government. We took our part in supporting the aspiration of our fellow countrymen, in the same way as we took part in supporting the nations of the world who fought for the right of small nationalities.

Who was Sir Henry Wilson? What was his policy, and what did he stand for? You have all read in the newspapers lately, and been told, that he was a great British Field Marshal; but his activities in other fields are unknown to the men of the British public.

The nation to which we have the honour to belong, the Irish nation, knows him, not so much as the British Field Marshal, but as the man behind what is known in Ireland as the Orange Terror. He was at the time of his death the Military Advisor to what is colloquially called the Ulster Government, and as Military Advisor he raised and organised a body of men known as the Ulster Special Constabulary, who are the principle agents in his campaign of terrorism.

My Lord and Members of the Jury, I do not propose to go into details of the horrible outrages committed on men, women and children of my race in Belfast and other places under the jurisdiction of the Ulster Government. Among Irishmen it is well known that about 500 men, women and children have been killed within the past few months, nearly two thousand wounded, and not one offender brought to justice.

More than 9,000 persons have been expelled from their employment; and 23,000 men, women, and children driven from their homes. Sir Henry Wilson was the representative figure and the organiser of the system that made these things possible.

My Lord and Members of the Jury, you can condemn us to death today, but you cannot deprive us of the belief that what we have done was necessary to preserve the lives, the homes, and the happiness of our countrymen in Ireland. You may by your verdict find us guilty, but we will go to the scaffold justified by the verdict of our own conscience.

Once Mr Justice Shearman had refused to read out that statement, both defendants withdrew their instructions from their counsel and no further defence was put forward. The jury having duly reached the only verdict really open to them, both men were then sentenced to death. Before he was taken down to the cells, O'Sullivan announced, 'You may kill my body, my Lord, but my spirit you will never kill.'

It has been said that in the days the two men spent in the condemned cell, they were subject to regular and brutal beatings from the prison staff. The truth of that can never, now, be verified but what is true is that O'Sullivan received a letter from a distant family member. That letter read:

I am proud of the honour of being a cousin of yours. It is with pride that I can hold up my head and say that I had a cousin who died for Ireland. It was a good day for Ireland the day yourself and your hero of a companion went out and laid the second Cromwell dead at your feet. You need not be afraid to meet your God.

On 8 August, the Irish government made an official request for mercy for the two killers. The plea was rejected out of hand. The fate of the two men was now sealed.

On the morning of Thursday, 10 August 1922, Joseph O'Sullivan and Reginald Dunne were hanged at Wandsworth prison by John Ellis, who was assisted by Edward Taylor and Seth Mills. Less than two weeks later, on 22 August, Michael Collins, the leader of the Irish Free State, was ambushed and shot dead in his County Cork home, by men who were against the IRA.

For many years, the bodies of the two men held as cold-blooded killers in England, and heroes in the Irish Republic, lay in unmarked graves in the prison where they died. However, in 1968, the bodies were exhumed and transferred to Ireland where they were reburied in Dean's Grange cemetery, in Dublin.

Chapter 29

George Frank Harvey
1934

George Frank Harvey had lived at the Westminster Poor Law Institute, at 367 Fulham Road, Chelsea, for some time. By April 1934, he had earned the respect of Harry Pocock, the labour superintendent of the institute, so much so that Pocock appointed Harvey as his batman. Amongst his other duties, Harvey would carry Pocock's meals to him each day, and clean his room. In order to carry out these duties, Harvey was given two keys to Pocock's rooms. He was also given a key to a storeroom, room B77, in the basement. It was there that he washed Pocock's plates after he had eaten, and where he kept various tools.

On Thursday, 25 October, Pocock saw Harvey a number of times during the day. He first saw him at 8.00am, whilst he was going about his duties. Pocock's final sighting of Harvey was at 4.50pm when he called into Pocock's room to see if he needed anything. Pocock said he was fine and Harvey then mentioned that he was going out for a couple of hours that evening.

The Institute had some rather strict rules for the inmates. Inside the building, all of them had to wear institute clothing, a sort of uniform, but they were forbidden from leaving, whilst wearing institute clothes. First, they had to ask permission to leave the building. If that were granted, they would be given a ticket and, just before they left, would sign for their outdoor clothes, change, and then check out at the main entrance.

Five minutes after Pocock had last seen Harvey; that is at 4.55pm, a bell rang. This was a signal to the inmates that it was teatime and that they should all report to the dining hall. This meant that at this time, all of B Block, would be empty of inmates.

At 5.15pm, George William James, the leave ward attendant, was in his office when Harvey reported to him with his exit ticket. By now he was wearing his outdoor clothing and, as was the custom, handed his institute clothing, in a bag, to James. The officer could not help but notice that Harvey was sweating profusely, as if he had been running, but thought nothing of this. Perhaps Harvey was just in a hurry to leave. However, before he could do so, James had to check that all the institute clothing was accounted for. James tipped the bag of clothing out onto the floor and checked it, only to find that a shirt was missing. James looked up, ready to confront Harvey about this, only to find that he had already gone.

Frederick George Oliver was another of the institute's attendants and on this particular day, he was on duty on the exit door. At around 5.20pm, the telephone in his office rang. When he answered it, Oliver found that it was George James, asking him not to let Harvey out of the building, until the missing shirt was accounted for. It was already too late. Harvey had shown his exit ticket and dashed out into the street.

Although room B77 was officially for Harvey's use, whilst it was not locked other inmates often went in there. One person in particular who used this room was George Hamblin, a close friend of Harvey's. Hamblin was the unofficial bookmaker for the other inmates and he took small bets on horse and dog races. He often operated this business from room B77 and it was there that the day's papers were taken to him, by William Richardson.

On 25 October, Richardson had taken the first newspaper to Hamblin, at 4.30pm. At that time Hamblin was in the storeroom, with Harvey, and they were discussing some bets. However, when Richardson took the second newspaper, at 5.30pm, he found that the door to the storeroom was locked, and that there was no answer when he knocked.

At some time between 10.30pm and 10.40pm that same night, 25 October, the labour master, Albert George Poole, checked all the beds in the institute. He found that two inmates were missing: George Harvey and George Hamblin. Both would be in trouble when they finally bothered to reappear.

The following morning, 26 October, at 7.05am, Albert Poole's shift was over and he was then relieved by the other labour master, Frederick Thomas. Mr Thomas was informed about the two missing inmates and decided to check the premises. One of the first ports of call was the storeroom, which both men were known to use. The door was still locked, but Thomas had a master key. He opened the door and even as he clicked on the light he almost lost his footing on something slippery. Looking down, Thomas saw a great deal of blood on the floor. He also saw the battered body of forty-eight-year-old George Hamblin. A bloodstained hammer lay nearby, and it appeared that the motive for this crime had been robbery, for Hamblin's trouser pockets were pulled inside out and their contents had been taken.

Although a full police search was launched for the missing inmate, Harvey, and details of the crime were published in the local newspapers, there was no real need for a manhunt for, at 2.10am, on Sunday, 28 October, Harvey walked into the police station at Paddington and gave himself up. He greeted the desk officer with, 'I'm Harvey. I understand you've been broadcasting for me.' He was then interviewed, by Inspector Ernest France, who charged him with murder later that same morning.

George Harvey's trial for murder opened on 21 January 1935, before Mr Justice Atkinson. The trial lasted until 24 January, during which time Harvey was defended by Mr FJ Eastwood. The Crown's case was led by Mr Eustace Fulton, assisted by Mr LA Byrne.

One of the first witnesses was Herbert Edward Hamblin of Sherborne in Dorset. He told the court that he had identified the body of his brother, at the Hammersmith mortuary, on 29 October. The dead man's full name was Allan George Hamblin, though he never used his first name. He had been born in Lambeth, in 1886.

Details of Harvey's movements on the day in question were then given. Arthur Burness Rose was the acting assistant manager of the institute, and he testified that at 9.00am, on 25 October, Harvey had asked him for a ticket to leave the premises. Originally he had only asked for a couple of hours, starting at 5.00pm. Rose had granted him a pass from 1.00pm until 8.00pm instead.

At 9.50am, Harvey was showing that pass to George Simpson, the senior receiving ward attendant. It was Simpson who handed Harvey his private, outdoor clothing, so he could change whenever he wished to leave.

Another part of the routine was that an inmate going out would also be issued with clean institute clothing. That would be left in his room so that when he returned, he could change out of his private clothing again, and put on a fresh, clean uniform. That was why the old one was supposed to be handed in. Richard George Barber handed the fresh uniform to Harvey at some time before 11.00am on 25 October. All clothing was marked and amongst the new clothing handed over was a shirt, which bore the mark B/132 on the inside of the collar.

Where had Harvey gone, after he had left the institute on the evening of 25 October ? The answer to that was provided by Clara Barnes who lived at 2 Colville Houses, Talbot Road, in Bayswater. She reported that she had first met Harvey in Hyde Park, some time in early September. They had soon become rather friendly and he had taken her to see a show.

On 24 October, Clara received a letter from Harvey saying that he had not forgotten her and asking to meet her on the coming Saturday, which was 28 October. He said he would be at the Regal cinema at Marble Arch at eight o'clock and hoped that she would condescend to meet him.

Clara did not reply to that letter, but she had intended to keep the suggested appointment. In the event, she was surprised to find Harvey at her house at some time before 5.45pm on 25 October. He explained that he was a bookmaker and had just lost rather a lot of money on a certain horse. Despite this he then gave her ten shillings, mostly in sixpence and shilling coins.

They discussed going to see a film and she had told him that she wanted to see one called *Manhattan Melodrama*. He agreed, but first they went for a walk to the Portobello market, where he bought her some grapes, before they went on to the Blue Hall cimema, back in Edgware Road. They bought two shilling circle seats and, like almost everything else that day, Harvey paid with a handful of silver coins.

At one stage, just after the film had started, Harvey excused himself, saying that he needed to use the toilet. He was gone for quite a long time and, when he returned to his seat, he immediately made it clear that he didn't like the film. Despite her protestations, he insisted they leave the cinema immediately.

From there, they went to a public house, *Finch's*, on the corner of Elgin Road and Portobello Road. Yet again more coins were brought out and at one stage Harvey asked the barman to change three shillings worth of coppers for him. They then went back to Clara's house and spent the night together. Clara woke up a number of times that night and each time she found that Harvey was sitting up in bed, smoking. He said he couldn't sleep and had something on his mind.

The next morning, they were both up at 6.00am. Harvey counted what money he had left and handed Clara a bloodstained postal order for 1/6d. He said that he had accepted it as payment for a bet he had taken. As he counted his money, Clara saw that he still had lots of small change and, curiously, a French 25 centime piece. He also had a key, which he said was to his large house in Wembley. He gave this to Clara for safekeeping, saying that he might lose it.

Later that day, Harvey bought a copy of the *Evening Standard* and mentioned that there had been a murder in the workhouse in Chelsea. That night they went to the Metropolitan Theatre, to watch a show, and then returned to Clara's house once again for the night.

The following morning, 27 October, Harvey admitted to Clara that he had been the man who had committed the murder. She was so shocked, that she fainted. When she came round, she begged him to go to the police, and said she would go with him if it helped. They decided to go to Hyde Park to talk things through and it was there that Harvey told Clara that if she went to the police he would kill her and then would kill himself. He added, 'They won't catch me alive.' She was terrified of what he would do and, after talking for hours, she agreed to go off on her own but said she would go back and meet him in the park at midnight. Instead she went straight home and bolted the door. She went to the police herself, the next day, not knowing that Harvey had already handed himself in.

Only three more witnesses were needed to tie up all the loose ends. Henry John Clarke worked at the Blue Hall cinema and he confirmed that he had found a bloodstained shirt in the gentlemen's toilets, on 26 October. The shirt bore the number B/132.

Walter Blanchett was another of the inmates at the institute, and he said that on 21 October, he had received a 1/6d postal order from his sister. He had given this to George Hamblin on 23 October, to cover a bet of 9d each way on a horse. Finally, yet another inmate, Charles Bushell, told the court that he knew that Hamblin kept a French 25 centime piece, as a good luck charm.

Giving his own testimony, Harvey claimed that the coins, which he had spent, had all been earned by him from selling cups of tea to the other inmates at a few pence a time. He went on to say that Hamblin had confided in him that he was being blackmailed. At one stage Hamblin had showed him a curious note which read, 'Yes, 13, Yes', but he would not say what it meant. However, none of this explained the bloodstained shirt, or his confession to Clara Barnes. The jury were far from satisfied and returned the expected guilty verdict. An appeal was entered and heard on 25 February, before Justices Avory, MacKinnon and Greaves-Lord. They found no reason to overrule the trial verdict and the appeal was consequently dismissed, and the death sentence confirmed.

At his trial, Harvey had revealed that this was not his real name. He claimed that he didn't want his family to know the trouble he was in, or that he had been living in poverty at the institute. It transpired that there were other things he had not wanted his family to know, including the fact that he had four previous convictions, all for stealing, and had served two terms of imprisonment, the last being a six months' sentence on 22 October 1929.

On Wednesday, 13 March 1935, thirty-seven-year-old George Frank Harvey was hanged at Pentonville by Robert Baxter and Henry Pollard. Only now did the authorities reveal that his real name had been Charles Malcolm Lake.

Chapter 30

Harold Dorian Trevor
1942

ixty-five-year-old Theodora Jessie Greenhall had lived in her flat at 71a Elsham Road, West Kensington, for some years, but now, in 1941, she was growing rather concerned about the German bombing of the capital. For her own peace of mind, she decided to move out of London and rent out her flat. With that in mind, in the autumn of that year, she contacted a local estate agent, Sladden, Stuart and Powell, of Royal Crescent.

On Monday, 13 October, the agent sent around a well-dressed and very polite gentleman who viewed the flat and said he was very interested in taking it. He arranged to call again, at 11.00am the following morning, for a second viewing.

On Tuesday, 14 October, the tall, distinguished man, with greying hair, did call again as he had promised. He even sported a monocle and, having been shown around the flat for a second time, said that he had fallen in love with it so much, that he would take it on the spot.

A few pounds were handed over as a deposit against the first month's rent, in order to fasten the deal and Mrs Greenhall then sat down at her bureau, in the drawing room, to write a receipt. She began, 'Received from Dr HD Trevor, the sum of ….'

The receipt was never finished for, as she wrote, the prospective tenant struck Mrs Greenhall over the head with a beer bottle. The bottle shattered into pieces, one large piece falling into a nearby waste-paper basket. Mrs Greenhall fell to the floor, unconscious, whereupon her 'tenant' fell upon her and strangled her to death with a ligature. He then ransacked the house, taking jewellery, money from a cash-box and some other items of value. As a final gesture, he placed a handkerchief over his victim's face.

Mrs Greenhall's body was discovered later that same day when her daughter from her first marriage, Miss Tattersall, paid her a visit. She called in the police and the case was put into the capable hands of Detective Chief Inspector Salisbury. He immediately called in the assistance of Scotland Yard and Detective Chief Superintendent Frederick Cherrell was sent to Kensington to assist.

Within a very short time indeed, Cherrell had all but solved the case, though he could not believe that the killer could have been so stupid. The partly completed receipt still lay upon the writing bureau and Cherrell read the name HD Trevor with interest. He knew of a petty criminal named Harold Dorian Trevor, who had spent most of the last forty years inside various prisons. In fact, sixty-two-year-old Trevor had only been free for a total of about eleven months, in the last forty years.

Trevor's prison career had started back in 1899. On 21 October of that year he had been sentenced to eighteen months in prison for stealing a dressing case. Eight other prison sentences followed, including one of five years in May 1905, one of seven years in July 1914 and one of ten years in August 1925. All had been for theft, larceny, stealing or false pretences. His last period of incarceration had started on 27 April 1936 when he received five years for larceny and receiving stolen goods.

Cherrell found it hard to believe that a killer would use his real name and then leave such incriminating evidence at the scene, so it was important that he check things out. He sent an officer to fetch Trevor's file and check up on his present whereabouts. As he waited, other officers found fingerprints on some of the broken glass, on a table top, and on the cash box.

Trevor's file duly arrived and, with the aid of a magnifying glass, Cherrell compared the fingerprints found at the murder scene, to those held on file. They were a perfect match, proving that the man who had leaned against that table, wielded the bottle and rifled the cash-box, was Harold Dorian Trevor. Further checks showed that Trevor had only finished his latest jail sentence a few days previously. In fact, he had been released from Parkhurst prison on 3 October, just eleven days before Mrs Greenhall had been killed. Finally, when the estate agent was spoken to, he confirmed that an appointment to view had been made in the name of Dr HD Trevor, of Devon. The hunt was on for the wanted man.

In fact, it soon became clear that Trevor had started on yet another of his crime sprees. The police soon discovered that on 9 October, Trevor had visited another estate agents, Harrods, of 62 Brompton Road. They had given him details of a flat at 8 Sloane Street and he had called there to see the owner, Beatrice Mary Haydock, that same day. At one stage she had left Trevor alone in one of the rooms and he had repaid her trust by stealing her handbag.

A check with the other estate agents in Royal Crescent, showed that Trevor had been given four addresses. In addition to the one at 71a Elsham Road, they had also given him details of properties at 42 Holland Road, 6 Norland Square and 9 St James Gardens. The owners of those properties were interviewed and all confirmed that Trevor had called on them on 13 October. His first visit, at 4.00pm, had been to St James Gardens, where he had agreed to take the flat but had not paid any deposit. At 5.15pm, he had visited Norland Square and less than an hour later, at approximately 6.00pm, he had visited Holland Road.

Back at Elsham Road, Mrs Tattersall was able to give the police details of the jewellery stolen from the house and the descriptions of the various pieces were circulated throughout the country. This tactic led police in Birmingham to report that two rings on the stolen list had been sold to a jeweller in that city. Trevor, it seemed, was moving north. Other pieces were traced to other shops, with the final piece being sold in Rhyl. Police in that town were told to be on the look-out for Trevor and this led to his arrest, on Saturday, 18 October, as he left a public telephone box.

Charged with murder, Trevor replied, 'It wasn't murder. There was never any intent to murder. I have never used violence on anyone in my life before. What came over me I do not know. After I hit her, my mind went completely blank and it is still like that now. Something seemed to crack in my head.'

Trevor's trial for murder opened at the Old Bailey, before Mr Justice Asquith, on 28 January 1942. During the two days of the hearing, Trevor was defended by Mr John Flowers and Mr Derek Curtis Bennett. The case for the Crown lay in the hands of Mr L A Byrne.

With the cast-iron evidence found at the murder scene, the defence did not try to deny that Trevor had claimed the life of Mrs Greenhall, but tried to persuade the jury that he must have been insane at the time of the attack. It was true that Trevor had an incredibly long criminal record, but all his previous offences had involved simple fraud and theft. He had never used violence before and its use in this case was completely out of character. The jury, however, chose to believe that Trevor was perfectly sane and, therefore, guilty of murder.

Asked if he had anything to say before the sentence of death was passed, Trevor made a long, rather flowery speech which, in part, said:

> *I would like, once and for all, to say this: that I, as a man who stands, so to speak, at death's door, would like to confirm all I have already said, regarding this lady's death. I have no knowledge of it.*
>
> *Even as I am speaking, the moving finger is writing on the wall, and the words, once written, can never be recalled. I sincerely hope that each of you, gentlemen of the jury, and the judge too, in passing sentence, will remember these words. That when each of you, as you surely must some day, yourself stand before a higher tribunal, you will receive a greater measure of mercy than had been meted out to me in this world. No fear touches my heart. My heart is dead. It died when my mother left me.*

Having finished his diatribe, Trevor was then sentenced to death by hanging.

An appeal was heard on 23 February, before Justices Humphreys, Singleton and Cassells, but they saw no reason to interfere with either the verdict or the death sentence. There was to be no reprieve and, on Wednesday, 11 March 1942, Harold Dorian Trevor was hanged at Wandsworth by Albert Pierrepoint, who was assisted by Herbert Morris. The forty-year crime spree was finally over.

Chapter 31

George Cyril Epton
1946

lbert Edward Stamp lived at 7 Billing Road, Kensington and, at 5.45am, on the morning of Monday, 6 May 1946, was on his way to work. Following his usual route, at one stage Albert walked down Finborough Road, and what he found there meant that he would certainly be late for work on this occasion.

Each of the houses down this street had steps leading up to the front door, with another set leading down to the basement. On the steps outside number 17, Albert found the body of a young woman. Her legs were on the top step and her head hung downwards, towards the basement. It seemed likely that she had fallen from one of the flats at 17 Finborough Road, and Albert could not help but notice that she wore no shoes. It was obvious that the woman was dead, but, rather surprisingly perhaps, Albert did not report the matter to the police. Instead, he found the nearest public telephone box and reported his find to St Stephen's Hospital.

It was the hospital who contacted the police and, at approximately 6.40am, Detective Inspector Albert Webb arrived to take charge of the scene. Looking up at the house it seemed that the most likely point of exit for the woman had been the flat on the first floor. This flat had a small balcony, directly overlooking the spot where the woman's body lay. It was probably the best place to start.

Webb walked into the house and went up to the first floor. The door was opened by a man, who greeted Webb with, 'I suppose you have come about the murder.' No mention of murder had been made and, indeed, the police were still not sure that this was a case of murder. 'What murder?' replied Webb. 'The one outside,' said the man. Webb was not prepared to go any further with that line, and demanded to know who occupied this particular flat. 'I do,' replied the man, who went on to identify himself as George Cyril Epton.

Inspector Webb said he was going to have a look around the flat, and Epton did not object. Walking over to the French windows, which led out onto the small balcony, Webb saw that they were fastened shut. Webb opened them and looked out, seeing what he believed were bloodstains on the stone floor.

'When were you out here last?' asked Webb. Epton said that he rarely went onto the balcony, except on hot days in the summer. 'Then how did these bloodstains get here?' continued Webb. Epton glanced at the stains and replied, 'That's not blood. That's dirt.' He then paused for a few seconds before adding, 'Well, they might be blood. My wife recently died of TB and she used to spit blood.'

Continuing his look around the flat, Inspector Webb entered the bedroom, and saw more stains, which looked like blood, on the bottom of the bed. Epton claimed that these stains were red ink. Then, after another pause, he admitted that they might be blood too, but claimed that if they were blood, then they were his blood as he had recently suffered a nose bleed. Inspector Webb said he was not satisfied with Epton's answers, and he would be taken to the police station for further questioning.

At the police station, Epton continued to say that he knew nothing of the dead woman. He had never seen her before, he did not know her and he certainly had had nothing to do with her death. Nevertheless, he was held in the cells overnight, whilst the police investigation continued.

By this time, the police had spoken to another resident of 17 Finborough Road, John Edward Eldred. He had returned home from work at some time between 9.00pm and 9.30pm on the evening of 5 May, and there had certainly been no body on the steps at that time. This proved that the woman must have been killed sometime on 5 May and her body dumped before 5.45am on 6 May. Meanwhile, items in the woman's handbag had identified her as Winifred Mulholland, who lodged at 8 Braemar Road, Brixton. When officers spoke to Winifred's landlady,

Lilian Hall, she confirmed that Winifred had been staying there for about eight weeks. She was also able to see that she had last seen Winifred at around 4.00pm on Sunday, 5 May, when she left the house. Later, Lilian made a positive identification of Winifred's body and also of the distinctive fur coat she had been wearing when she left Braemar Road.

Back at the police station, later that same day, 6 May, Epton was asked for a full statement outlining his personal details, and his movements over the last few days. He began by saying that he had lived at the flat for six years, initially with his wife. She had died, from consumption, on 24 February, since which time he had lived there alone. He had been unemployed since the end of February, and before that, had been an engineer's assistant at Fulham Cross.

Epton then turned to his movements on the days preceding Winifred Mulholland's death. He gave a timetable, which involved visits to the Labour Exchange, meeting a lady friend in Tottenham Court Road, and taking her to the pictures. On the Sunday, the day Winifred had last been seen alive, Epton said he had walked to the Kings Road in Chelsea, and had a drink in the *Six Bells* public house, but had been home in bed by 10.30pm.

At around 4.00am, on the morning of Monday, 6 May, Epton had been woken, by someone ringing the bell of the house next door. A minute or two later, his own front door bell rang and he heard voices in the street outside, but could not distinguish what they said. This was followed by the sound of a car racing off, after which it went quiet. He went back to sleep and knew nothing of the crime until someone knocked at his door and the police came in to talk to him.

Epton was then asked to explain a few things that did not add up. The dead woman had been wearing no shoes when she was found. A pair of women's shoes had been found in Epton's fire grate, partly burned. Black, with red sides, Epton claimed that they had belonged to his wife and he had put them on the fire because they were of no use now. For the time being, the police decided that they had questioned Epton enough and he was returned to the cells.

In the early hours of 7 May, Epton asked to speak to a senior police officer. Divisional Detective Inspector John Ball went to see Epton, who then made a further statement, admitting that he had been involved in Winifred's death. He was then charged with murder.

Epton's trial on that charge took place at the Old Bailey, before Mr Justice Birkett, on 16 June 1946. During the two days that the proceedings lasted, Epton's defence rested in the hands of Mr Malcolm Morris, whilst the case for the prosecution was led by Mr Anthony Hawke, assisted by Mr Henry Elam.

The body of Winifred Mulholland had been examined by Professor Donald Teare. Called to the scene in Finborough Road at 10.00am on 6 May, Teare had performed the post-mortem later that same day.

Professor Teare reported a series of circular shaped abrasions on Winifred's body. One group were on her right cheek and another two were on her left. There were similar wounds around the chin and left eye. All of these wounds could have been caused by a hammer found inside Epton's flat.

Continuing his evidence, Professor Teare detailed an irregular shaped wound, four inches across, in the centre of Winifred's forehead. There was another wound at the back of her head and these could have been caused by an iron, again found in Epton's flat. These wounds had fractured Winifred's skull, causing a corresponding laceration of the brain, which was the direct cause of death. Considerable violence must have been used.

Winifred had sustained even more injuries after she was dead. There was a wound on the front of the throat, bruises on the knuckles of her right hand and other bruises on the fingers of her left hand. Her neck vertebrae had been fractured and the lower end of one thigh bone was broken. These wounds could have been caused by a fall onto the steps from the first-floor balcony.

Dr James Stanley Higgs had been the first doctor on the scene on 6 May. He had confirmed that life was extinct. The following day he had taken blood samples from the dead woman and also from Epton. Both samples had been sent to the police laboratory.

Walter Eric Montgomery was a Senior Scientific Officer at the

Metropolitan Police Laboratory at Hendon. He had examined various articles taken from Epton's flat. Blood had been found on some linoleum, and there were signs that this had been swabbed by something in an attempt to clean it up. There were bloodstains and hairs adhering to a flat iron, but he had found nothing of value on a hammer. A rug, also taken from the flat, was heavily bloodstained at one corner. All the stains were of type A, but tests had shown that both Winifred and Epton had blood of that type.

Of more value were hairs and fibres taken from various locations. On the bloodstained rug, Walter had found three dyed rabbit hairs, and these matched hairs taken from Winifred's distinctive coat. Similar hairs were found on the stonework above the portico outside 17 Finborough Road, and the ironwork around the balcony. Dyed rabbit hairs, and bloodstains, were also found on Epton's trousers.

Epton's second written statement was then read out. In this he admitted that he had met Winifred at around 10.00pm, on 5 May, in Piccadilly. They fell into conversation and he asked her if she would like to come home with him. She accepted, saying that she had nowhere else to go.

Back at the flat, Epton claimed that they then had sexual intercourse, on a chair, after which he went to his bedroom. Whilst there, he noticed that £9 was missing from his hip pocket. Going back into the living room, Epton demanded to know if Winifred had taken his money. She said that she hadn't but she was grinning as she denied it. At this, Epton grabbed her, reached out for something, and struck her on the head. She fell and it was plain that she was dying. Rather than go for help, Epton then dragged her into the bedroom and left her there before going into his kitchen and making himself a cup of tea. Later, he had gone back into the bedroom and found that Winifred was dead. He left her there that night and later that morning, pulled her back into the front room where, at about 4.00am, he put her over the balcony.

With all the evidence against him, and his own confession, there could be no doubt as to the verdict. Found guilty, Epton was then sentenced to death. This was, in fact, the first death sentence awarded since the House of Commons had voted to abolish capital punishment, a vote that was subsequently overturned by the House of Lords.

In fact, Epton never did hang. On 20 July, his sentence was commuted to one of life imprisonment. He was, of course, the second man to have killed in Finborough Road. Ronald True had murdered Gertrude Yates, twenty-four years earlier, at number 13a, just a couple of doors away from where Winifred Mulholland had died.

Chapter 32

Thomas John Ley
and Lawrence John Smith
1946

On Saturday, 30 November 1946, Walter Thomas Coombes left his home to gather some firewood from the nearby Chalk Pit woods, in Surrey. On his way back home he decided to go via the chalk pit itself, and turned onto a track close to Limpsfield Road, in Hamsey Green, just north of Warlingham.

Walter had not gone very far, when he spotted a bundle of rags in a small trench. Curious as to what the bundle might be, Walter walked towards it and, the closer he got, the more he thought that someone had dumped a tailor's dummy in the woods. However, as he reached the bundle he realised that this was no dummy. It looked very much like a man's body. Walter ran home to tell his father what he had found.

Walter's father was also named Walter Thomas Coombes, and he took his son back to the woods to investigate further. Walter senior saw the bundle for himself and still wasn't sure if it were a man's body or not. At one stage he crouched down, lifted one of the trouser legs very slightly and touched the leg of the bundle. Now there was no doubt. Walter had felt cold human flesh. There was a body in the woods. Walter returned home with his son, and telephoned the police.

Constable Cyril Victor Hearn arrived at the woods at 4.30pm. He began by taking a close look at the body. The man, whoever he was, lay on his right side with his legs protruding from the end of the shallow trench. His left forearm rested on the edge of the trench. The man's head was encased within a grey tweed overcoat. His left arm was still in the sleeve of this coat but his right arm was out, and the coat had then been twisted around and over his head.

Looking closer still, Hearn saw that the man had a length of rope wound twice around his neck. Perhaps this was a case of suicide. The man might have hung himself from a nearby tree, and after his death, the rope had snapped, and his body had rolled down the small hill and landed in the trench. That might also account for the coat being wound about his head.

It was obviously important to identify the dead man and Constable Hearn now made a careful search of his pockets. In one pocket, Hearn found a blue Freemasons membership card, and this gave the name John McMain Mudie. Other papers gave an address. Apparently Mr Mudie had been staying at the *Reigate Hill Hotel*, in Reigate itself.

The police officers investigating the case visited the hotel, and gave a description of the dead man. That confirmed that the dead man was indeed John Mudie. Margaret Kinniburgh Park was the owner of the hotel, and she confirmed that Mudie had worked at the hotel, since May. Originally he had been taken on as a night porter, but in due course had been asked to help behind the bar. By the time of his death he had been put in charge of the bar. He had grown to be friendly with one of the assistants at the hotel, a Miss Phoebe McGill, and seemed to be happy enough. Margaret knew of no reason why Mudie would have taken his own life.

A check was made on any telephone calls, which Mudie had made, and the log showed that on 22 November, Mudie had telephoned a John William Buckingham, of Marlborough Place, St John's Wood. A search of his room revealed two letters, concerning some cheques that needed to be returned, from a firm of solicitors named Denton, Hall and Burgin of 3 Grays Inn Place, London. One of those letters had been sent to Mudie at the hotel, but the other had been addressed to him at 3 Homefield Road, Wimbledon.

The next stop was the solicitor's office in Grays Inn Place. They confirmed that they had written two letters to Mudie. The first had been sent to his lodgings in Homefield Road and, when he had moved to the hotel at Reigate, a second letter was sent there. These letters had been written on behalf of one of their clients, a company named Connaught Properties Limited, the chairman of which was a gentleman named Thomas John Ley.

Thomas Ley was something of a famous figure. He had been born on 28 October 1880, in Bath, but his father had died when he was very young, and his mother then took him and her three other children to Australia, arriving there in 1886. After leaving school, Ley had first worked as an assistant in his brother's grocery shop, but later became a clerk in a solicitor's office in Sydney. He had shown a keen interest in politics and, in 1917, Ley became a member of parliament in New South Wales.

In 1922, Ley became the New South Wales Minister for Justice. By 1925, he was a member of the Federal House of Representatives, but during the elections of that year, a curious thing had happened. Ley had offered his Labour opponent, Frederick McDonald, a bribe of £2,000, being a share in a property, in return for withdrawing from the ballot. McDonald refused the offer and, after Ley had won the election, decided to make the details of the attempted bribe public. However, the case collapsed when McDonald mysteriously vanished, never to be seen again.

There were also other curious incidents in Ley's past. One political opponent had fallen from cliffs near Sydney, another had fallen overboard from a ship and drowned. All these might well have been coincidences, but there were some who said that Ley had organised these 'accidents'. Whatever the truth of that, Ley was defeated in the 1928 election and decided to return to England with his mistress, Maggie Evelyn Byron Brook.

By now, the police had determined that Mudie's death was not a case of suicide. If, as had been believed, his body had rolled into the ditch, then his clothing would have collected leaves, dirt, grass and other debris from the floor of the woods. No such items were found. Mudie's suit was pristine apart from the mud stains from the ditch itself. This was confirmed at the post-mortem when it was shown that no vertebrae had been broken as would have resulted from a drop. Mudie had died from asphyxia. He had been slowly strangled. It was clear that he had been killed elsewhere and his body then dumped in the woods.

The investigation continued and the police could not help but notice that Maggie Brook, Ley's long-time mistress, lived in one of the flats at 8 Beaufort Gardens, where Mudie had once lived. This gave a second link between Ley and Mudie but, as yet, there was no strong evidence. The police, however, did have one lead.

In the days before he had last been seen at the *Reigate Hill Hotel*, Mudie had spoken to other members of staff about being invited to a cocktail party by a well-to-do woman. She had, apparently, been in the bar with her chauffeur and had fallen into conversation with Mudie. An invitation had been made and he was now only waiting for the date to be confirmed. He had, however, told the woman that the best day for him would be a Thursday, as that was his regular day off. Apparently, the woman, and her chauffeur had indeed called, at around 7.00pm on Thursday, 28 November. Mudie had not been seen alive since that date. Could this woman and her servant have been involved in his murder? Yet again, there was no hard evidence on the matter, and neither of the people could be traced.

The newspaper reports had given all the details of the investigation thus far, and everyone who read the stories knew that the police were looking for the elegant woman and her chauffeur. The police were also regularly questioning two people; Ley himself and John Buckingham, a man who Mudie had telephoned from the hotel. It was that pressure which finally led to a break in the case.

At 5.55pm, on Saturday, 5 December 1946, three people walked into the offices of Scotland Yard, and announced that they had some information on the body found in the chalk pit in Surrey. The three were forty-three-year-old John William Buckingham, his twenty-one-year-old son who had the same name, and Lilian Florence Bruce.

Buckingham senior said that some six weeks ago he had been in the *Royal Hotel* in Southampton Row, London, when a porter he knew said that there was a man who wanted a job done, and would pay handsomely for it. Buckingham explained that he did not wish to be involved in anything illegal, but the porter said it was nothing like that. Buckingham said he would like to know more and, in due course, the porter introduced him to Mr Ley.

Ley explained that he was a retired solicitor, but still looked after the financial interests of two women. One of these was a Miss Brook, and she was being blackmailed by a man. That man, Mudie, was now living at a hotel in Reigate, and Ley wanted nothing more than to talk to him, and offer him £500 to stop his illegal activities and leave the country.

Two days after this, another meeting was arranged, at which Ley introduced a man named Smith, who he said worked for him as a builder's foreman. He would help Buckingham to bring the man to one of Ley's flats at 8 Beaufort Gardens, where he and Smith would make him the offer of money for his silence. The trouble was that Mudie would not just climb into a car with two strange men. Some subterfuge was necessary, and it was Buckingham who came up with the idea of using the attractive Lilian Bruce, a friend of his, to invite Mudie to a cocktail party.

The plan was put into action, and Mudie agreed to go to the party. The pick-up was made on Thursday, 28 November, with both the Buckinghams, Miss Bruce and Mr Smith going to fetch Mudie, and bring him back to London. Once they were at the flat, Miss Bruce and the younger Buckingham left, and the other two escorted Mudie into the flat. There he was seized, trussed up with a rope and left inside the flat. Buckingham senior then left, having been paid £200 for his trouble. He believed that the roping of Mudie was just to frighten him into accepting the offer, but now he knew that Ley and Smith must have murdered Mudie and dumped his body in the Surrey woods.

With this information, the police made three arrests. John William Buckingham had been directly involved in tying Mudie up, so he was arrested as an accomplice to murder. Ley was arrested and charged with murder and the Smith referred to in the story was identified as Lawrence John Smith, a man who worked for Ley. He, too, was charged with murder.

Now that the police had all the story and the names of all those involved, they could determine the real reason for this terrible murder. It was nothing to do with blackmail, though it was all about Maggie Brook, Ley's mistress. It transpired that although she now lived in Beaufort Gardens, Maggie had once lodged at 3 Homefield Road, the same address that Mudie had lived at. Ley had managed to convince himself that some sort of sexual relationship had taken place between Mudie and Maggie, and that was the reason he wanted Mudie dead.

In due course, the charges against Buckingham were dropped, especially as his evidence would be crucial for the prosecution. That left Ley and Smith to face their trial together. That trial was due to start on 26 February 1947, before Mr Justice Hilberry, but the defence argued that they were not ready to proceed and the hearing was put back to March.

Eventually, both men were found guilty of murder and sentenced to death. An appeal was heard, on 21 April, before Lord Justice Oliver, Mr Justice Atkinson and Mr Justice Cassells. That appeal was lost and the death sentence confirmed. Both men were due to hang on 8 May 1947.

In fact, neither man did hang. Smith's sentence was commuted to one of life imprisonment, whilst Ley was adjudged to have been insane at the time of the murder, and was then committed to Broadmoor. He died there very shortly afterwards, on 29 July 1947.

Chapter 33

John George Haigh
1949

I n the autumn of 1898, John Robert Haigh married Emily Hudson in Wakefield. That fact has led a number of authors to erroneously believe that their only child was also born in Wakefield. In fact, a few years after they had married, the Haighs moved to Stamford in Lincolnshire and it was there, on 24 July 1909, that Emily gave birth to a son, who they named John George.

It can be said that a number of factors would eventually fashion the emotional make-up of John George Haigh. It is true that in later years, Emily would say that during the latter part of her pregnancy, she had felt very nervous and anxious. There is also the fact that John Robert Haigh was out of work, perhaps adding to that anxiety. Added to this, it should be noted that both John Robert and Emily were members of the Plymouth Brethren, an Evangelical Christian movement, and they believed that the world was an intrinsically evil place. They determined that their son would be protected from such evil, and their beliefs were reflected in his upbringing.

Fortunately, whilst John George Haigh was still a baby, his father found work in Yorkshire and the family moved to Outwood, near Wakefield. Here they brought up their son in a most strict manner, forbidding him from mixing with other children and building a high fence around their back garden, so that he could play there, free from the influence of others. No radio or newspaper was allowed in the house and Bible stories were the order of the day. Haigh was, however, quite a bright boy and he later won two scholarships; one to the Queen Elizabeth Grammar School in Wakefield and one to Wakefield Cathedral, where he became a choirboy.

During these formative years, the fear of God's wrath was drilled into Haigh. His father had a blue mark on his forehead, caused by an accident in his youth. He told his son that he had sinned and this was the mark of Satan, put there for all the world to see. As for his mother, well, she was free from such blemishes, showing that she was a pure angel and should be treated as such.

Although he was a bright boy, Haigh could not be bothered to apply himself. It is true that he won three prizes; one for geography and two for divinity, but he also discovered a talent for forgery. He would copy his teacher's handwriting and pen his own glowing school reports, finding that to be much easier than applying himself to his studies. The truth about his academic achievements came when he took his school certificate, and failed.

After leaving school, Haigh took a position as an apprentice to a firm of motor engineers, but a life of hard physical toil was not to his liking. Other, less grimy positions followed, in insurance and advertising, but in 1930, when he was twenty-one years old, Haigh was dismissed after being suspected of stealing some cash from a money box. He had, by now, discovered that if he lied, or stole, or committed some other crime, then God's wrath didn't strike him down or mark him for life. His belief in religion was waning and Haigh began to think that he was invincible and could get away with anything.

On 6 July 1934, just before his twenty-fifth birthday, Haigh married twenty-one-year-old Beatrice Harmer, a union he would later say was nothing more than a marriage of convenience so that he could escape his parent's influence. The relationship was not a happy one from the outset and soon afterwards, Haigh was arrested for a fraud he had committed, by selling cars that he didn't actually own. For that offence, on 22 November 1934, he was sentenced to fifteen months in prison. During his incarceration, his wife gave birth to their child, a daughter, who was immediately put up for adoption. Beatrice then took the opportunity to leave her husband and it would be fifteen years before they set eyes on each other again.

On his release from prison, Haigh moved to London where he took a position as secretary and chauffeur to William Donald

McSwann, a wealthy owner of a number of amusement arcades. Haigh had not, however, settled down to a life of honest industry for he soon set up as a bogus solicitor and started perpetrating a fraud involving vehicles bought on hire purchase, which he then sold for cash. He was eventually caught and charged and, on 23 November 1937, almost three years to the day since his last court appearance, Haigh received another prison sentence, this time for four years.

In 1941, Haigh was freed from prison and took a job as an accountant with an engineering firm. Soon after this, on 10 June 1941, he received his third prison sentence, one of twenty-one months, for looting and theft from bombed-out houses. It was during this period that Haigh, determined that he would never go back to jail, began to study the law, reading book after book on the subject. He managed to convince himself, erroneously, that if the police did not have a body, then there could never be a charge of murder brought against a killer. He therefore decided that when he was released, he would be better off embarking on a career of murder for gain because, as long as there was no body, a murder could not be proved. The problem was, that he needed to find a way of disposing of the body so that no trace would ever be found. Then, one day, he found the solution.

Haigh worked in the prison workshop where he had access to equipment and chemicals. One of those chemicals was sulphuric acid and, having found a dead mouse, Haigh proceeded to experiment by placing the small body into a container of acid. To his delight, he found that the body dissolved within thirty minutes. Obviously, a fully-grown human being would take far longer than this but here, at last, was the way to make a body disappear and, with no body, there could surely be no charge of murder. It seemed to be the perfect crime.

Released from jail in 1944, it was later that same year that a chance encounter led to Haigh putting his plan for that perfect murder into operation.

In the late summer of 1944, Haigh called into *The Goat* public house on Kensington High Street, for a quiet drink. There, by pure coincidence, he bumped into his ex-employer, William

Donald McSwann. The two fell into conversation and McSwann took Haigh back to see his parents, William and Amy, at their top-floor flat, 45 Claverton Street, Pimlico. They made the mistake of telling Haigh that they had recently done a lucrative property deal and had a good deal of money in the bank.

Haigh spent the next few weeks ingratiating himself with the McSwann family and, one day, William Donald intimated that he was rather concerned that he would be called up to fight in the war. Haigh said he thought he might have the solution to his problem and also told McSwann about a new pin-ball machine he claimed to have invented. Haigh then invited McSwann back to a basement, which he had rented at 79 Gloucester Road, also in Kensington, to look at the machine and discuss his options on avoiding a call-up. There, on Saturday, 9 September 1944, whilst McSwann's back was turned, Haigh bludgeoned him to death and disposed of his body.

Haigh would later tell conflicting stories of how he managed this task. In some he claimed that he simply used a meat mincer to grind the body into minute pieces which he then flushed down the drain. In another variation, Haigh claimed that he placed McSwann's corpse inside a forty gallon drum which he then topped up with sulphuric acid. Eventually, McSwann's body was reduced to a sludge, which Haigh then tipped down the drain in the middle of the basement. Whichever method he actually did use, Donald McSwann's body was completely disposed of.

Haigh now took the opportunity to move into William Donald McSwann's house.

Haigh explained, to his victim's parents, that their son had gone into hiding in Scotland, to avoid being called up, and had asked him to look after the house in order to deter burglars or looters. For a time the McSwanns believed everything, especially when they received letters from their son; letters which Haigh had forged. Eventually, however, as the war drew to a close, it was clear that McSwann would have to make a reappearance and, when he did not, his parents would ask some rather awkward questions. Indeed, they had already started to wonder why Haigh was disposing of some of Donald's assets. Haigh decided that the best course of action was to remove them as well.

William and Amy McSwann were last seen alive on 2 July 1945. Haigh would later admit that he lured them, separately, to the basement at 79 Gloucester Road where he battered them to death before putting the bodies into tanks filled with acid. Once they had dissolved, they too were flushed down the drain. After this, Haigh used his forgery skills to obtain the title to the McSwanns' houses, businesses and other property owned by them. In all, he made around £8,000 from the murders, a considerable sum in 1945, worth about £208,000 pounds today. It was also about this time that Haigh moved to the *Onslow Court Hotel*, on Queen's Gate, in South Kensington, where he occupied room 404.

For some years, Haigh lived in comfort at the hotel, but in due course, most of the money had gone, due mainly to the fact that Haigh was a gambler, but not a very good one. By early 1948, financial concerns meant that another victim needed to be found; a victim with money.

Dr Archibald Henderson was a very successful man, with property, money and a good position in life. He and his attractive wife, Rose, lived in a large house in Dawes Road, Fulham. They had recently converted their previous property, at 22 Ladbroke Square into flats and were in the process of advertising them for sale. One of the potential buyers who saw that advertisement was John George Haigh.

Posing as a prospective customer, Haigh visited the flats and even made an offer on one of them. The deal, naturally, fell through, but Haigh had been so charming and plausible that the Hendersons decided to keep in touch with him. They even told him when they were going on a short break to Brighton, staying at the *Metropole Hotel*. Haigh said that he would join them and booked his own room in the same hotel.

By this time, Haigh had given up the basement in Gloucester Road and had begun using a storeroom at Leopold Road, Crawley. This actually belonged to a man named Edward Charles Jones, who ran a company named Hurstlea Products. Jones and Haigh had first met in 1935 and Jones was fully aware of Haigh's talent for inventing mechanical devices. Jones even gave Haigh an unpaid position as salesman and offered him the use of the storeroom at Leopold Road, which Haigh told people was his 'factory'. Ostensibly, the storeroom would be used for industrial experiments, but Haigh had more nefarious plans for the building.

On 16 February 1948, Haigh lured Dr Henderson to the factory in Leopold Road where he shot him dead, with Henderson's own gun, which he had stolen from his house in Dawes Road. Haigh then returned to Brighton and informed Rose Henderson that her husband had been taken ill at Crawley. The kindly Haigh even offered to drive Rose to Leopold Road, so that she could be with her husband. Once there, she too was shot, both bodies being then dissolved in acid.

This was to be Haigh's most successful killing to date. Using his forgery skills he managed to convince the Henderson's family and servants that the couple had gone to South Africa. It was well known that the Hendersons had had their own marital concerns and Haigh's explanation that they had gone abroad, to make a fresh start was readily accepted. He then went on to appropriate their property, earning himself another £8,000 or so.

It was not until the following year that Archibald Henderson's brother became concerned. He asked the BBC to make an appeal for his brother to return home, but so plausible and glib had Haigh been that the brother believed that if anything had happened to Archibald and his wife, it must have taken place in South Africa. Once again, no one suspected the charming and debonair Haigh of any involvement in the disappearance.

By now, Haigh had murdered five people in as many years, and obtained property which today would be worth around half a million pounds, but it was still not enough. His considerable debts, mostly through gambling losses, had swallowed most of that money so that, later in 1949, he was again in dire financial straits. His hotel bill was unpaid and a cheque he had just written out for £32 5s 5d to cover that bill, would undoubtedly bounce when it was presented to his bank. This duly occurred and Haigh was now told that he must settle his bill, in cash, at the very earliest opportunity.

On Wednesday, 16 February 1949, Haigh paid his hotel bill in full. It had now risen to £49 18s and Haigh, as the hotel had requested, paid it in cash. In fact, the day before, 15 February, Haigh had borrowed the sum of £50 from Edward Jones at Crawley. However, Jones had told his friend that he must have the money back by the coming weekend at the very latest, as he had an insurance premium to pay. Haigh had paid one debt by raising another and since he had less than a week to pay this money back, time was now running out for him.

One of the other guests at the *Onslow Court Hotel* was a lady by the rather grand name of Olive Henrietta Helen Olivia Robarts Durand-Deacon. Mrs Durand-Deacon had been a resident of the hotel for some two years and she was interested in a new business venture. She had had the idea of producing false fingernails and needed someone to give her some advice on how this might be achieved. She knew that Haigh was something on an inventor and had approached him with the idea. He had said that he might be able to assist her and invited her to come with him to his factory in Crawley, once he had made up some prototypes. An arrangement was made, and the date for the visit set for Friday, 18 February 1949.

That same night, a friend of Mrs Durand-Deacon's, another guest named Constance Lane, noticed that she did not come down for dinner at her usual time. This might not have been a cause for concern, but Mrs Durand-Deacon was a creature of habit and it was certainly not like her to be absent without some sort of explanation.

The following morning, at some time between 9.00am and 10.00am, Haigh had approached Miss Lane, whilst she was enjoying her breakfast and asked if she had seen any sign of Mrs Durand-Deacon. When Miss Lane said she had not, Haigh reminded her of the appointment he had made with her the previous day. He then claimed that Mrs Durand-Deacon had said she was just going to the Army and Navy Stores in Victoria Street and asked him to meet her there. He had arrived at the store at 2.35pm, but there had been no sign of Mrs Durand-Deacon, so he had driven down to Crawley alone.

By the following morning, 20 February, Olive Durand-

Deacon had still not appeared and Haigh again approached Miss Lane, to see if she had any news of her friend. Not only had Constance heard nothing, but she had now grown so concerned that she told Haigh she must go to the police and report her disappearance. At first, Haigh seemed to be a little concerned, but he had certainly recovered his composure a couple of hours later, when he returned to Miss Lane and said that he would go to the police station with her. That same day, Olive Durand-Deacon was reported as a missing person at Chelsea police station.

On Monday, 21 February, Divisional Detective Inspector Shelley-Symes, called at the *Onslow Court Hotel*, as a matter of routine, to interview Haigh. Asked for further details of the appointment they had had, Haigh was only too happy to supply what details he could. He pointed out that the last time he had actually seen the missing woman was at 1.50pm on the 18th, when she had told him where she was going. He had waited for her outside the store, but when she hadn't appeared after an hour or so he simply assumed that she had changed her mind and so went to his workshop in Crawley by himself. After doing some work there, he had enjoyed a meal in a local hostelry, before leaving Crawley at around 7.00pm.

Inspector Shelley-Symes thought that there was something rather too glib about the charming Haigh and decided, again as a matter of routine, to run a police check on him. This revealed Haigh's criminal record and his three prison terms. It made such interesting reading, that the inspector decided to dig a little deeper.

A talk to Hilda Kirkwood, the book-keeper at the hotel, brought forward the information that one of Haigh's cheques had recently bounced, but that he had settled his bill with £49 18s in cash on 16 February.

The next step was to look at the workshop in Crawley. Since the premises actually belonged to Hurtslea Products, the police visited their offices, in West Street, Crawley first. There they spoke to Edward Jones, who confirmed his relationship with Haigh and also that he had lent him £50 on 15 February, the day before Haigh paid his hotel bill.

Jones was also able to say that on 17 February, Haigh was back at West Street and asked Jones if he could take the leg off a stirrup pump for him. Jones did as his friend asked, assuming that the pump was needed for one of Haigh's experiments. At the same time, Haigh mentioned that he was bringing someone down from London to look at an idea for producing false fingernails. Jones held the keys to the premises at Leopold Road and Haigh arranged to pick them up the next morning.

On the morning of 18 February, Haigh arrived at Crawley very early. Jones had to collect some steel stored at Leopold Road and Haigh took him down there in his car. The steel was loaded and it was Haigh who then took the keys, and locked the doors. Later that same day, Jones saw Haigh again, and was told that Haigh's potential business partner had not turned up for their meeting. He had, however, repaid £36 of the money he owed.

Where had Haigh obtained that £36? He had been so short of cash that he had had to borrow money from his friend to pay his hotel bill, but now he suddenly appeared to be in possession of a good deal of cash. Perhaps there was some sort of clue at Leopold Road. So it was that on 26 February, Detective Sergeant Patrick Heslin entered the storeroom and began a search of the premises.

There were a number of interesting items in the storeroom. Heslin noticed three large carboys containing sulphuric acid, standing in the centre of the floor. On the bench nearby lay a rubber apron and a pair of rubber gauntlet gloves, as well as an Army-type respirator or gas mask. The stirrup pump Edward Jones had referred to was propped up against a wall and on another bench, in the far corner of the room, was a square, leather hat box, which was locked.

Sergeant Heslin also found some papers, which he thought might be of interest. One of these was a receipt, from a dry cleaners in High Street, Reigate. This appeared to be for a fur coat. What on earth was Haigh doing with a hat box and a fur coat? The items were taken away as possible evidence and later that same day, when officers visited the premises in Reigate, and spoke to Miss Mabel Marriott, they found that the fur coat had been brought in by a well-dressed and very charming gentleman. Miss Marriott said that she would be unable to positively identify the gentleman, but she did produce the fur, a Persian lamb coat of the type Mrs Durand-Deacon had been wearing when she disappeared on 18 February.

On 28 February, Inspector Shelley-Symes was back at the *Onslow Court*, this time accompanied by Detective Inspector Albert Webb. They asked Haigh to go with them to Chelsea police station, so that he might clear up a few matters. Haigh was more than happy to oblige. There, questioned again about Mrs Durand-Deacon's disappearance, Haigh kept to much the same story as before, until faced with the evidence of the fur coat left at the Reigate cleaners. Haigh fell quiet and seemed to be considering his position.

After some time in custody, Haigh was left alone with Inspector Webb. After remaining silent for a few minutes more Haigh suddenly asked, 'Tell me frankly, what are the chances of anybody being released from Broadmoor?' The remark shocked Webb and he replied, 'I cannot discuss that sort of thing with you.'

Haigh was not to be stopped now and continued, saying, 'Well, if I tell you the truth you would not believe me. It sounds too fantastic for belief.' He then paused before adding, 'Mrs Durand-Deacon no longer exists. She has disappeared completely and no trace of her can ever be found again. I have destroyed her with acid. You will find the sludge that remains at Leopold Road. Every trace has gone. How can you prove murder if there is no body?' Later, when Inspector Shelley-Symes returned, Haigh made a full written statement describing in detail how he had killed and disposed of Olive Durand-Deacon.

Despite the fact that they now had a confession, the police needed more to prove that a murder had been committed. They also had to prove that the victim of that murder was none other than Olive Durand-Deacon, and that the person responsible was John George Haigh. With that in mind, Dr Keith Simpson, the pathologist, visited the alleged murder scene on 1 March.

One of the first things Simpson noticed was that on the whitewashed walls, between the two windows, was a group of what appeared to be blood spatters. Scrapings of those stains were taken for further analysis. Outside, some 475lbs of dirt, the entire top soil to a depth of three or four inches, was loaded into wooden boxes and taken back to the laboratory for examination. Meanwhile, the locked hat-box was forced open, to reveal a Webley revolver, which had recently been fired.

Back in London, Simpson carefully sifted, sieved and separated the soil and this revealed a number of incriminating items. First, there was the handle of a red plastic handbag. Such a bag, missing its handle, had been found in the yard, dumped behind a pile of bricks. Tests would show that the broken handle fitted that bag and Mrs Durand-Deacon had been seen with just such a bag on the day she vanished.

Other items found in the sludge and soil included a set of upper and lower dentures. These were examined by Lily Patricia Mayo, a dental surgeon of New Cavendish Street, London. Mrs Durand-Deacon had been a patient of hers for more than twenty years and Miss Mayo had made her at least five sets of dentures in that time. She was able to confirm that this was the last set she had made, in 1947.

Continuing his search, Dr Simpson found 28lbs of a very greasy substance which he later identified as some sort of animal fat, possibly human. There were also three gallstones and eighteen fragments of human bone. Not only was Dr Simpson able to piece together some of those bone fragments, to show that they were female, but he was also able to say that the owner was in late adult age as they showed signs of arthritis. Olive Durand-Deacon would have been sixty-nine on 28 February.

Other scientific minds were brought to bear on the case. Dr George Turfitt, the deputy director of the Metropolitan Police laboratory, examined the inside of a large green metal drum that had been found in the workshop. He found a considerable quantity of what proved to be animal fat and also traces of sulphuric acid.

Dr Henry Smith Holden, the director of the same laboratory, made an examination of the fur coat found at the dry cleaners in Reigate. The bottom of the coat and one of the sleeves had been patched and he found that portions of fabric found inside the red plastic handbag matched the material used precisely. He also found traces of human blood on the respirator case, the rubber apron and amongst the whitewash scrapings taken from the walls.

Charged with murder, Haigh made his first appearance at a court convened in Horsham Town Hall on 2 March. The details of the charge were given and, after a hearing of just five minutes, Haigh was remanded to 11 March. The police, meanwhile, were investigating other missing persons, whom Haigh said that he had killed. On 3 March, officers visited the basement at 79 Gloucester Road, South Kensington. Again samples of soil were taken and by 4 March, the story had broken in newspapers across the world. One newspaper, though, went too far.

No fewer than three editions of the *Daily Mirror* had been published on 4 March and each issue carried banner headlines about John George Haigh. At this time, Haigh had only been formally charged with one murder and, in all probability, evidence would only be heard on that one crime, as is common in British courts. The *Daily Mirror*, though, had published details of six possible murders and had given details of Haigh's claims that he had drunk the blood of his victims, stating plainly that he was a vampire killer. This could be highly prejudicial to the case and as a result, on 8 March, Haigh's legal representatives made an application to the King's Bench Division Court for leave to apply for a writ of attachment against Mr Silvester Bolam, the editor of the newspaper. The case was eventually heard on 25 March, before the Lord Chief Justice, Lord Goddard and Justices Humphreys and Birkett. So seriously did they view the articles, that they fined the newspaper proprietors £10,000 and jailed Mr Bolam for three months. On the same day, Haigh, who had also been remanded on 11 March and 18 March, was further remanded to 1 April.

It was on 1 April that the evidence was finally detailed at Horsham. The initial hearing would last for two days, evidence being heard only on the one charge, that of the murder of Mrs Olive Durand-Deacon.

The prosecution began by stating that Haigh had lived at the

Onslow Court Hotel since 1945. Over the last couple of years he had taken his meals at a table next to that of Mrs Durand-Deacon, so it was quite natural that they should get to know each other.

Evidence was given that on 7 February, Haigh's personal bank account at the Gloucester Road branch of the Westminster Bank, had been overdrawn by £83 5s 10d. By 23 February, only £5 had been paid in, so it was clear that this account was not a source of funds and if Haigh needed money, he would need to resort to other methods of obtaining it.

On 17 February, Haigh had purchased the large 45-gallon drum he would need in order to dispose of his victim's body. The following day, he and Mrs Durand-Deacon left for Crawley in his motor car at around 2.00pm. When they arrived they had first visited the *George Hotel*, where they both used the toilet. The couple were seen by the hotel's book-keeper, Hannah Caplin. She knew Haigh as a regular customer and was able to identify his companion as Olive Durand-Deacon from a photograph shown to her by the police.

According to Haigh's own detailed statement, they had then gone down to the workshop, where Mrs Durand-Deacon was shown some papers, supposedly relating to the manufacture of fingernails. As she turned towards the windows in order to see better, Haigh stood behind her, levelled his revolver at her head and put a single bullet into her brain. He then removed her fur coat and jewellery and put the body, along with the rest of her belongings, into the 45-gallon drum.

Haigh decided that he had worked hard enough for the time being and needed a break from his efforts. He went back to Crawley town centre where he entered The Ancient Priors, a restaurant, and enjoyed a cup of tea and some poached eggs. He then returned to Leopold Road where he filled the drum with acid. He then returned to the *George Hotel*, where he had dinner, before leaving for London at around 9.00pm.

On 19 February, Haigh returned to Crawley via Putney. On the way he stopped at a jeweller's, Barrett and Sons Limited, in the High Street where he spoke to Herbert Louis Richmond to whom he offered an 18-carat diamond and ruby wrist watch. Haigh, who used the name F Miller, asked for £15 for the watch but finally settled for £10.

Arriving back at his workshop in Crawley, Haigh inspected the drum of acid and found that the reaction was not yet complete; a large piece of the dead woman's buttocks were floating on top of the sludge and grease. Having topped up the acid, Haigh picked up the fur coat, which had been lying on a bench, and travelled on to Horsham, where he had the rest of the jewellery valued. On the way, he stopped off at Reigate and left the fur coat at the cleaners.

On Monday, 22 February, Haigh was back at Crawley where he saw that the chemical reaction was almost complete. There was a good deal of sludge floating on the top so Haigh emptied this off with a bucket and dumped it in the yard. He then topped up the tank with acid and returned to London.

On Tuesday, 23 February, Haigh sold the rest of the jewellery for £100. In fact, he only took £60 that day, as the jeweller did not have sufficient cash on the premises. He picked up the remaining £40 the next day. Meanwhile, he returned again to Crawley, where he emptied the tank into the yard. He also visited Edward Jones and paid him back some of the money he owed him.

Having heard all the evidence, the magistrates sent Haigh for trial at the next sessions at the Old Bailey, which were due to open on 26 April. Haigh's case actually came up on the 27th, before Mr Justice Humphreys.

The defence asked for permission to defer the case to the next sessions, claiming that they were not yet ready to proceed. Mr Justice Humphreys made it clear that he believed the case should not even have been sent to London in the first place. Whilst it was true that Haigh had admitted committing three murders in Kensington, the evidence of the one case that would be heard, was on a murder in Sussex and should, therefore, be tried by a Sussex jury. The judge sent the case back to Sussex, to be heard at the next Lewes sessions. These were due to open on 11 July.

Haigh's trial actually opened at Lewes on Monday, 18 July, and lasted for two days. Although Mr Justice Humphreys had returned the case from London, it was that same gentleman who presided over the Sussex assizes and so it was he who heard the evidence against Haigh. For the prosecution, Sir Hartley Shawcross led, assisted by Mr Gerald Hayward and Mr Eric Neve. Haigh's defence lay in the hands of Sir David Maxwell Fyfe, who was assisted by Mr GRF Morris and Mr David Neve, the son of Eric.

Although evidence on only one crime would be heard, Haigh had actually confessed to nine murders. In addition to William Donald McSwann, William McSwann, Amy McSwann, Archibald Henderson, Rose Henderson and Olive Durand-Deacon, Haigh also claimed that he had killed a woman he had met in Hammersmith, a young man he had met the same year, and a woman named Mary who he had met at Eastbourne. It must be remembered, though, that Haigh was a master liar and, relying on a defence of insanity, was claiming as many victims as he could.

Once Haigh's detailed confession had been read out in court, and the evidence on the murder of Mrs Durand-Deacon heard, the time came for the defence to put forward their case. The only possible defence, as suggested by Haigh himself, when he mentioned Broadmoor, was one of insanity. The defence called Dr Henry Yellowlees, a psychiatrist, who had examined Haigh on three occasions in Brixton prison.

Dr Yellowlees began by detailing Haigh's strict religious upbringing and his failed marriage but then moved on to Haigh's story of his dreams and lust for blood.

Haigh claimed that ever since he had been a young child, he had been fascinated by blood. His mother was in the habit of chastising him, when he misbehaved, by rapping him across the back of the hand with a hairbrush. This often caused his hand to bleed and he had sucked the blood and found the taste agreeable. From that time on he had taken to hurting himself deliberately in order to taste the blood. Haigh had also told Dr Yellowlees of two recurring dreams that he had had since childhood.

The first of these was a dream of Christ on the cross, blood pouring from his wounds. The second, which Haigh called the 'tree dream', was more sinister. In this, a forest of crucifixes slowly turned into trees from which rain appeared to be dripping. A dark figure collected this 'rain' in a chalice and it soon became clear that the rain was actually blood. The dream would end when the figure offered the chalice up to Haigh with an invitation for him to drink.

For some years, these dreams and the urges they produced in Haigh were suppressed by him, until one day in 1944, when he was involved in a road accident near Three Bridges in Sussex. Haigh's head was cut in the accident and the blood ran down into his mouth. This had rekindled his desires and led to him committing murder in order to drink the blood of his victims. His confession detailed how he made an incision, usually in the neck, of each of his victims, drew a glassful of blood, which he then drank down with relish.

Dr Yellowlees stated under oath that in his opinion, Haigh was a lunatic and, although he may have lied about drinking the blood, he almost certainly carried out this ritual and may well have tasted some blood from each victim.

The jury retired on the second day and took just seventeen minutes to decide that Haigh was perfectly sane, and therefore guilty of wilful murder. It was announced, by his defence team, that there would be no appeal and they would instead rely on the medical evidence to obtain a reprieve for him.

The Home Secretary, Mr Chuter Ede, immediately set up a panel of medical experts to examine all the evidence in great detail. Eventually they presented their own conclusions: they agreed with the jury that Haigh was sane and guilty as charged.

On Wednesday, 10 August 1949, a crowd of some 500 people gathered in the bright sunshine outside Wandsworth prison. At 8.30am a telegram was delivered to the prison. Half an hour later, at 9.00am, John George Haigh was hanged by Albert Pierrepoint, assisted by Harry Kirk, who gave him a drop of seven feet four inches. Pierrepoint used a special calf-leather wrist strap to pinion Haigh's hands behind his back, a strap he only ever used in cases where he had a special interest.

Chapter 34

John O'Connor
1951

Eighty-two-year-old Eugenie le Maire had lived at 15 Perham Road, West Kensington for many years. Occasionally she would rent out rooms to lodgers but, in the autumn of 1951, there was just one man living with her: twenty-nine-year-old John O'Connor. Eugenie treated her lodger well, and looked after him almost like her own son.

On the evening of Saturday, 11 August, John O'Connor walked into his local police station and admitted he had killed his landlady. Taken in for interview, he then made a detailed written statement outlining what he had done. O'Connor then handed over his front door key and, after officers had visited the house in Perham Road, was charged with murder.

O'Connor's trial took place at the Old Bailey on 2 October 1951, before Mr Justice Barry. The case for the Crown was outlined by Mr Christmas Humphreys, and O'Connor was defended by Mr W Hemming.

In fact, O'Connor actually faced two trials on that day. The first was to decide on his ability to understand the charge and enter a plea. Once that jury had decided that O'Connor knew what he was doing and could fully understand the proceedings, a second jury was sworn, to hear the evidence on the charge of murder.

In this rather unusual case, there were no witnesses to what had taken place inside 15 Perham Road. The prosecution began, therefore, by reading out O'Connor's statement to the police.

O'Connor stated that on the night of 10 August, he had visited several public houses and freely admitted that he was quite drunk by the time he took a taxi back home. He arrived quite late, but Eugenie had still not gone to bed, and kindly said that she would make him a cup of tea. O'Connor then followed her into the kitchen and then, whilst she was pottering about with the kettle, he suddenly seized her by the throat and tried to strangle her. She struggled for a while and then slipped into unconsciousness.

O'Connor's statement conveniently missed out the next part of what had happened to Eugenie le Marie. He claimed that he had immediately gone upstairs. Later medical evidence would show that actually, at this point, O'Connor raped his landlady, before going up to his bedroom.

Continuing his narrative, O'Connor said that he had been in his bedroom for a short time, thinking about what he had done. Rather than feeling any remorse, he then went back downstairs, to find that Eugenie was still unconscious on the floor. After looking at her helpless form for a few moments, he then calmly walked across the room, picked up a large bread knife and stabbed Eugenie repeatedly in the heart and lungs. He then washed, before walking to the police station and giving himself up.

At the beginning of the trial, the judge had explained that there were only three possible verdicts in this case. The first was guilty of murder, the second was not guilty, and the third was guilty but insane. Given the detailed written confession to the crime, O'Connor's barrister had expressly stated that the only possible defence was one of insanity. O'Connor, however, would have none of it. He expressly forbade Mr Hemming to bring forward any evidence as to his state of mind.

As a result of this, Mr Hemming could do very little to try to save his client. O'Connor even refused to step into the witness box to try to explain his actions. This meant that not only could the defence not rely on a plea of insanity, but they could also call no witnesses and could offer no evidence whatsoever, as to why O'Connor may have committed this terrible crime.

The jury, having heard the police and medical evidence and O'Connor's detailed confession, took only ten minutes to return their verdict. O'Connor was guilty of murder. There could, of course, be only one outcome, and O'Connor was duly sentenced to death.

Even now, O'Connor did nothing to try to save his own life. He did not enter an appeal and refused to have his solicitor plead for the sentence to be commuted to one of life imprisonment. As a result of that, on Wednesday, 24 October, just twenty-two days after he had been sentenced, John O'Connor was hanged at Pentonville, by Albert Pierrepoint and Harry Allen, for what was a totally motiveless and senseless crime.

Chapter 35

Dennis George Muldowney
1952

Krystyna Skarbek was a true heroine. Born in Poland on 1 May 1908, she was the daughter of a Count and grew up to marry Jerzy Gizycki, on 2 November 1938. Soon after this, Jerzy was sent to Ethiopia as a Consul and the couple were there, in Addis Ababa, when Hitler invaded Poland, on 1 September 1939.

Krystyna and her husband made their way to England where, soon afterwards, their marriage failed. Eager to fight in some way against the German invaders of her home country, Krystyna travelled to Hungary, where she met an old acquaintance, Andrzej Kowerski. Free from her husband, Krystyna fell in love with Andezej, who was just as determined as she was to fight against the Germans. In due course, they made contact with a group calling themselves the Musketeers, who decided that the couple could work for them. In all, they made three undercover visits to Warsaw, in order to collect valuable information for the Resistance, which they in turn sent on to London.

On the return to Hungary from their third visit to Poland, Krystyna and her partner were arrested by the Hungarian Secret Police, but they managed to escape. As experienced operatives, they then contacted the British Ambassador, Sir Owen O'Malley, who arranged, amongst other things, false British passports for them. From this time onwards, Krystyna would use her new anglicised name, Christine Granville.

Christine continued to work as an operative and sent back information from Turkey, Egypt and Palestine. It has been said that the information which she sent back to London enabled Winston Churchill to predict that Hitler was about to invade Russia.

From Egypt, Christine joined the Special Operations Executive. Transferred to Algiers she travelled by plane to France, where she landed, by parachute, on 6 July 1944. Soon afterwards, on 13 August, her commanding officer was arrested by the Gestapo, along with a major and a French officer. Held in a prison in Digne, they would, almost certainly have been executed, but Christine walked into the prison, claimed to be married to one of the prisoners and to be a niece of Field Marshal Montgomery. She then calmly informed the prison guards that she would make sure that they were all shot as war criminals if they harmed any of the prisoners.

After the war was over, Christine's war service was recognised by many of the countries she had served. She was awarded the George Medal by Britain, the Croix de Guerre avec Palmes, by France, and also a medal from her native Poland. She was also given an OBE. There was, however, one problem: Christine could not settle after the war and found it hard to find a position that suited her.

For a time she worked as a saleswoman, in the dress department at Harrod's store in London, whilst she lived at the *Shelbourne Hotel*, situated at 1 Lexham Gardens, Kensington. When that didn't work out she took a job as a telephonist at India House, followed by a spell as a cloakroom attendant at a different hotel. Finally she took a new role, as a stewardess on a ship, the *Winchester Castle*, travelling between Britain and Australasia.

In May 1951, Christine travelled to the docks in London to join her latest ship, the *Ruahne*, which was about to sail. As she struggled up the gangplank with her heavy suitcase, a small, smiling man stepped forward and offered to help her. The man identified himself as Dennis George Muldowney and he said that he was a bathroom steward on the same ship. A friendship developed, which was to last until February 1952.

Though Muldowney would later claim that his relationship with Christine Granville was a full-blown, mutual love affair, it is highly likely that this was not the case. It may well be true that Muldowney fell hopelessly in love with the distinguished war heroine but, for her part, Christina saw him as a friend, nothing more.

After the ship had completed its round trip to New Zealand, Christine returned to London. Muldowney followed and on one occasion, he and Christine went to see a film at the cinema. Unfortunately, Christine brought along another friend, a man, and Muldowney managed to convince himself that this other man was obviously Christine's lover. By now she had realised that Muldowney was obsessed with her and, in April 1952, she told him, in no uncertain terms, to leave her alone. Indeed, she refused to tell Muldowney where she was staying in London, and broke off all contact with him.

Muldowney was not to be dissuaded and determined on a course of action that would lead to tragedy. He bought himself a knife and a rubber cosh and began searching for Christine. He had decided that he would kill her and then take his own life by poisoning himself. Finally, in order to give himself time to find her, Muldowney left his job on the ships and took a position as a porter at the Reform Club in Pall Mall, London.

There were a number of location where Christine was known to frequent in London, including a Polish club. To Muldowney's dismay, however, she seemed to be avoiding those places and it was by pure chance that he eventually discovered that she was staying at the *Shelbourne Hotel* in Kensington. On Sunday, 15 June 1952, Muldowney bumped into a mutual friend, who told him where Christine was living. It was time to put the murder plan into operation.

That same night, Christine went out for a meal with some friends. She had just decided to leave England and join Andrzej Kowerski, now known as Andrew Kennedy, who was living in Brussels. Her intention was to travel to Belgium the very next day. It was some time before 10.30pm by the time she got back to the hotel.

Josef Taduesz Kojdecki was one of the hall porters in the hotel and he was on duty that night. He heard someone coming into the hotel and, looking around, saw that it was Christine. He heard her running up the stairs, and, just two or three minutes later, saw a man enter the hotel. He would later identify this man as Dennis Muldowney.

Kojdecki went into the office for a minute or so and, when he came out, he saw that Christine had come back downstairs and was in the hallway, talking to Muldowney. Their conversation was none of Kojdecki's business so he carried out with his work.

In the hallway, Christine had found Muldowney waiting for her. He stood in front of her, blocking her way, and asked if she would give him back the letters he had written to her. Christine said she was unable to do so, as she had burned them all. She then repeated that she did not want anything more to do with him, and asked him to leave her alone. She then went on to say that she was leaving Britain the following day. Muldowney asked her how long she would be away and she replied that she would be gone at least two years. Without a further word, Muldowney took out the new shiny knife he had purchased, and plunged it into Christine's chest.

Christine's dying scream brought two of the hotel porters rushing to her aid. One, Kojdecki, seized Muldowney and held him fast whilst his companion, Michal Perlak, telephoned for the police. It was all too late for Christine. The heroine of the Second World War lay dead on the floor of the *Shelbourne Hotel.*

Having heard all this commotion, the hotel manager, Bronislaw Antoni Hryniewicz, came to see what all the noise was about. He saw Christine, lying on the floor, with a knife embedded in her chest, up to the hilt of the handle. Bronislaw took the knife out and threw it onto the ground. He also brought some water and tried to get Christine to take some but it was clear that she was dead.

By the time Inspector Leonard Pearcey arrived at the hotel, it was 10.40pm. He found Muldowney being held, on the stairs, by Kojdecki and Perlak. Pearcey was with Constable Priest and Constable George Yarnold and the three officers escorted Muldowney into the lounge of the hotel. Having examined the scene and determining that Christine was dead, Pearcey said to Muldowney, 'The lady is dead. What happened?' Muldowney replied, 'That's the idea. I did kill her. She drove me to it. It is my knife.'

A few minutes after this, Constable Yarnold was guarding the prisoner when he saw Muldowney take a silk handkerchief out of his pocket and put it to his lips. There was a glint behind the material and Yarnold saw that Muldowney was trying to take some white powder from a bottle. The officer knocked Muldowney's hand away, and confiscated the bottle.

Muldowney was held at the hotel for some time, while the police examined the scene. It was not until 2.45am on 16 June that Chief Inspector George Jennings arrived, to take charge of the prisoner. Told that he would be charged, Muldowney would only reply, 'I killed her. Let's get away from here and get it over quickly.'

Muldowney was escorted to the police station and charged with murder. The following day, 16 June, Dr Francis Edward Camps performed the post-mortem on Christine, at Kensington mortuary. He reported a single stab wound, some five-eights-of-an-inch long, below the top of the breast bone. The wound was five inches deep and had cut the heart itself. Christine would have been dead before her body hit the floor of the foyer.

Forty-one-year-old Dennis Muldowney faced his murder trial on 10 September 1952, before Mr Justice Donovan. The case for the prosecution was due to be led by Mr Christmas Humphreys but, in the event, his services were not required. Asked how he wished to plead to the charge, Muldowney replied, 'Guilty.'

The learned judge asked Muldowney if he were fully aware of the consequences of such a plea and advised him to seek legal representation. Muldowney said that he knew precisely what the consequences were, and confirmed that he did wish to plead guilty. Given every chance, to at least try to save himself, Muldowney persisted in saying he was guilty. He was then sentenced to death and as the judge intoned the final words, '...and may the Lord have mercy on your soul'. Muldowney replied, 'He will.' The entire trial had lasted just three minutes.

Afterwards, the newspapers of the day were able to reveal something of the history of Dennis Muldowney. Born in Wigan, he had apparently had parents who were rather too fond of drink. There was no suggestion that they had mistreated their children, but Dennis had grown into a weak boy, who was frightened of the dark and of being alone. He had married in 1929 and had one son, but his wife divorced him in 1947 on the grounds of his cruelty. Apparently his sexual demands were too great, with Dennis often demanding sex three or more times each day. The wife had since remarried and her son, now twelve, knew nothing of his real father.

Muldowney refused to enter an appeal or to petition for the death sentence to be lifted. Nor did he show any remorse for what he had done. In a final letter, dated 11 September, Muldowney wrote to his brother James, who lived at 64 Caunce Street, Wigan. In that letter he said, 'She asked for what she got.'

In the condemned cell, Muldowney could not have been described as a model prisoner. He showed contempt for his jailers, thinking them beneath him. He refused to get out of bed in the mornings, and often had to be forcibly dressed by the guards. He refused to go out on exercise, and complained that the food was of low quality.

On Tuesday, 30 September 1952, Dennis George Muldowney was hanged at Pentonville by Albert Pierrepoint, assisted by Herbert Smith. He had been given a drop of seven feet, three inches. In fact, this was a double execution, Muldowney being hanged alongside Raymond John Cull, who had murdered his wife, Jean Frances Cull, in Northolt, Middlesex, on 29 June.

Andrzej Kowerski, the man Christine had been planning to go to when she was killed, lived until 1968. He never married and, when he died, was cremated and his ashes were scattered near Christine's, in London, at the Catholic St Mary's cemetery. Finally, they were together.

Chapter 36

Kenneth Gilbert
and Ian Arthur Grant
1954

There were two senior porters at the *Aban Court Hotel*, situated at 25 Harrington Gardens, in Kensington, and these two men took turns to do the night-shift. The first of these, John David Downey, was on the day-shift during the week beginning Monday, 8 March 1954 and he finished work, each evening, at 8.30pm. It was then that the other porter, fifty-five-year-old George Smart took over.

Mary Magennis, a chambermaid, had worked at the *Aban Court* for the past two years. On 9 March, she had the afternoon off, but arrived back at the hotel at 10.45pm. As she went up to her quarters, she greeted George, who was sitting at the reception desk, reading a newspaper.

A few minutes after this, at 10.50pm, the manageress of the hotel, Ethel Maud Robertson Bryston, also saw George at the reception desk. She too bade him a warm goodnight before going up to her rooms.

On that particular Monday, the other porter, Downey, who also lived in at the hotel, decided that he would go out for a few drinks, after he had finished his shift. He returned to the hotel at 12.58am on Tuesday, 9 March, by which time, as was usual, all the doors were locked. Downey rang the front door bell and was admitted by George Smart. The two men exchanged goodnights and Downey then went up to his bed.

Mary Magennis's alarm clock went off at 7.00am on the morning of 9 March. She got dressed quickly and was downstairs at some time between 7.15am and 7.30am. She went straight into an area known as the servery and noticed, to her surprise, that the lights were still off. She quickly snapped them on and the sight that greeted her put all thoughts of work from her mind. There, on the floor, lay the bloody body of George Smart.

The manageress, Ethel Bryston, was called for and, after seeing the awful scene for herself, rang for the police. Later, acting on police instructions, Ethel made a careful inventory of items that were missing and, during the period that she was making her notes, she found a man's cap in the porch behind the front door. That cap did not belong to any of the hotel staff.

Two police officers arrived at the hotel together. Constable Harold Roumph and Constable Mace took charge of the scene, until more senior officers could arrive. They noted that all the hotel doors were still locked.

The police investigation soon showed that George Smart had opened the front door to a female guest at approximately midnight on 8 March. Of course, he had been seen alive almost one hour later, by John Downey, so it was obvious that the attack upon him had taken place after that time. It also became clear that the killer, whoever he was, had gained access by forcing a door into the coal cellar. The presumption was that Smart had disturbed the would-be thief and been battered to silence him. He had then been tied up and gagged and later, a post-mortem would show that the actual cause of death was asphyxia.

Though theft had been the motive, the thief had not been a very successful one. A large quantity of cigarettes had been taken, but there was only £2 1s 9d in cash, which had been inside a drawer, and this had been forced open by means of a screwdriver. All the areas around the murder scene were dusted for prints but nothing was found, apart from prints that were to be expected to be there, such as the other members of staff. It looked like this might be a difficult case for the police to solve.

In fact, it turned out to be nothing of the sort. Later that same day, a man named Donald Stuart Chapman walked into Waltham Green police station, with a left-luggage ticket. Chapman explained that he was working at Olympia, in connection with the forthcoming Ideal Home Exhibition. The ticket had been given to him by two men, who also worked there. They had confessed that they had robbed a hotel, killed a man and put the cigarettes they had taken into the left luggage office at Victoria station. They had asked Chapman to pick the cigarettes up and keep them at his house until the weekend. Chapman had agreed, but had then gone straight to the police instead. Finally, he gave the names of his two co-workers: Kenneth Gilbert and Ian Arthur Grant.

A record check showed that both Gilbert and Grant were already known to the police. Grant, who had been born on 9 May 1932, had four previous convictions for larceny, shopbreaking, stealing and assault. Gilbert, born on 30 December 1929, had just one conviction, for stealing a car.

After officers had collected the stolen property from Victoria, and checked out Chapman's story, they decided to make the necessary arrests. At 1.00pm on 10 March, Detective Superintendent William Judge, Detective Inspector Victor Massey, and a number of uniformed officers, travelled to Olympia. The first person they found was Gilbert who, when told that he would be arrested on a charge of murdering George Smart replied, 'I don't know anything about it.' Very soon afterwards, the officers approached Grant who, to the same charge retorted, 'I don't know what this is all about.' Both men were then taken to Chelsea police station where, later that day, both made statements incriminating the other.

The trial of Gilbert and Grant took place on 10 May 1954, before Mr Justice Glyn-Jones. Mr Christmas Humphreys and Mr Mervyn Griffiths-Jones detailed the case for the prosecution. Gilbert's defence lay in the hands of Mr John Hazan, whilst Grant was defended by Mr Peter Crowder. The proceedings would last until 12 May and, in addition to murder, both men were charged with larceny.

Dick Harness was a kitchen hand at the hotel. Part of his job was to clean up the servery area and he had done this on 8 March, during which time he left a kitchen cloth on a shelf in the room. After the murder, and once George Smart's body had been moved, Harness cleaned the servery again. By now the cloth was missing. Later medical reports would show that this cloth was the one forced into Smart's mouth, to silence him.

John Woodward was the head porter at the *Aban Court* and had been there for six and a half years. He had checked the petty cash box and saw that there were some odd coppers scattered on the floor, close to the now empty box. In all, once this money had been taken into account, there was the sum of £2 1s 9d missing.

Margaret Helen Edwards was the hotel's head receptionist and part of her duty was to maintain stocks of cigarettes. On the morning of 8 March, she had checked the stock. There were two unopened packs of 200; one of Weights and one of Piccadilly. There were also packets of Players, Capstan and Churchman and, in all, some 700 cigarettes were missing by 9 March.

Dr Jacob Arthur Gorsey had been called to the hotel at 8.10am on 9 March. He confirmed that George Smart was dead and, from temperature comparisons, calculated that the time of death had been at around 2.00am.

William Edward Winkley was a cab driver and he was on duty during the early hours of 9 March. At some time after 2.00am, Winkley was on the cab rank outside the *Buckingham Hotel* in Cornwall Road, when two men walked up to his cab from the direction of the *Aban Court*.

One of the men asked him to drive them to Kings Road. Winkley did as he was asked, dropping them just over the Stanley Bridge. One of the men got out immediately and walked off in the direction of Harwoods Road. The other paid the fare with two half crowns before running after his companion. Having heard of the murder, Winkley had approached the police and had since made a positive identification of Gilbert and Grant.

Harry Walter Humphrey, was a leading porter at Victoria station and, on 9 March, was working in the left luggage office from 6.00am until 2.00pm. Very soon after he had come on duty, a man had left a small wooden case with him. He had given the name Grant, and this name had been written on his ticket. Humphrey also made a positive identification of Grant as the man he had seen. He was present when police officers opened the box and saw that it contained a lot of cigarettes, including two unopened packs of 200.

One of the most important witnesses was Donald Chapman, the fellow worker Gilbert and Grant had confided in. The first man to approach him was Grant who early on 9 March admitted that he and Gilbert had 'done a job' in a hotel and got themselves a few cigarettes. Later that morning, Gilbert had approached him, with the *Star* newspaper. He showed Chapman the article on the murder and said, 'Don, what do you think I've done? I've done somebody in. I didn't mean to do it. What shall I do?'

For the rest of the morning, both Gilbert and Grant spoke to him a number of times about the robbery. Then, at around noon, one of them mentioned that the cigarettes were at Victoria station. Grant handed over the ticket and asked him to go to Victoria and collect the cigarettes. Chapman had, of course, taken that ticket to the police.

After telling the court about the arrests, Detective Superintendent Judge spoke of events at Chelsea police station. He had interviewed Grant, who at one stage said, 'I told Gilbert not to keep hitting him. When he showed me the paper and I saw the old man had died, I realised what we'd done.'

At the same time, Inspector Massey was interviewing Gilbert. Massey told the court that right at the beginning of the interview, Gilbert had said, 'I suppose he's down there talking his bloody head off. I never should have taken him with me. You can get your pen out and start writing. I'll make a statement and it will be the truth.'

In those statements, both men admitted playing a part in George Smart's death but each blamed the other for the actual murder. Gilbert, who had once worked at the *Aban Court Hotel* for three months in 1953, admitted that he had struck Smart, but had only hit him twice before gagging him. Grant, for his part, claimed that he had seen Smart with his hand raised, as if he were about to strike out, and so hit him once, in the stomach. It was Gilbert who then hit Smart very hard, and continued to beat him, even after he was tied up.

The jury had little trouble in finding both men guilty of murder. There was now no need to proceed with the larceny charges and they were dropped. Both men were then sentenced to death.

An appeal was entered and during the proceedings the defence claimed that, since neither man had gone to the hotel with the intention of killing Smart, the correct verdict should be guilty of manslaughter. The three appeal court judges ruled that since the men had gone to the *Aban Court* with the intention of stealing, and were quite prepared to use violence, the charge was one of murder. The appeal was dismissed.

On Thursday, 17 June 1954, Kenneth Gilbert and Ian Arthur Grant were hanged at Pentonville by Albert Pierrepoint, who had three assistants: Royston Rickard, J Grant and Harry Smith. Though other pairs of killers would be hanged in the future, this was the last time that two men were hanged side by side at the same time. From this time onwards, double executions were always carried out at two different prisons.

Chapter 37

Guenther Fritz Erwin Podola
1959

On Friday, 3 July 1959, a burglary took place at a flat in Rowland Gardens, South Kensington. The owner of the flat, a model named Verne Schiffman, lost some furs, jewellery and personal papers. In all, the value of the haul was put at £2,000, a considerable sum of money at this time.

A few days after the robbery, on Tuesday, 7 July, Mrs Schiffman received a letter, which purported to come from an American private investigator named Levine. In the letter, Mr Levine claimed that some letters and tapes, of a compromising nature, had come into his hands. Mr Levine would be happy to give these items back to Mrs Schiffman, for the sum of £500.

Verne Schiffman knew full well that no such incriminating tapes or letters existed and that this was nothing more than a crude attempt at blackmail. Further, since this had all occurred within a few days of the robbery, it seemed reasonable to assume that the caller was the man who had burgled her flat. Mrs Schiffman contacted the police.

On 12 July, Verne Schiffman received a telephone call from someone who gave his name as Fisher, and said he was acting as an agent for Mr Levine. Fisher wanted to know what her reply was to Mr Levine's offer. An astute Mrs Schiffman asked the caller to ring the next day, contacted the police again, and had a trace put on her telephone line.

At 3.30pm on Monday, 13 July, Fisher rang back as he had been asked. Verne Schiffer kept the man talking while the police traced the call. Within minutes they had discovered that the caller was ringing from a public telephone box at South Kensington underground station. Mrs Schiffman was still talking to the potential blackmailer when she heard him shout,

'Hey, what do you want?' This was followed by the sound of a scuffle and then a new voice came onto the line. The voice said, 'Mrs Schiffer, this is Detective Sergeant Raymond William Purdy. Remember my name.'

In fact, two police officers had rushed to the telephone box in South Kensington. Purdy had been accompanied by Detective Sergeant John Sandford and they now began to escort the arrested man out of the underground and into the street. As they did so, the man managed to squirm free and run off down the street. The two sergeants gave chase and saw him vanish into a block of flats at 105 Onslow Square.

There was no other way out of the building, so it was now only a matter of time before the two detectives spotted their quarry. Within moments, he was seen trying to hide behind a concrete pillar. He was ordered to come out and not try to get away again.

Sergeant Purdy sat the man down on a low window sill while his colleague went to find the caretaker of the flats. Sandford knocked on the caretaker's door but there was no reply. As he turned to tell Purdy, the man they had arrested reached into his jacket pocket, took out a revolver and fired one shot at Sergeant Purdy.

Detective Sergeant Raymond William Purdy fell to the floor, a bullet in his heart. As Sandford dashed to help his stricken colleague, their prisoner escaped for the second time. Sergeant Purdy was already dead. The burglary and blackmail suspect was now wanted for murder.

Two days after the shooting, on 15 July, Sergeant Purdy's widow rang the police station. After her husband had been killed, officers had, as was routine, called around to offer their deep condolences and to return her husband's property to her. One item, however, an address book, did not belong to her husband and Mrs Purdy was at a loss to know how it had been mixed up with Raymond's possessions.

The notebook did not belong to Raymond Purdy, but it had been found in his jacket pocket when he had been shot. Since it did not belong to him, it seemed reasonable to assume that it must have belonged to the man that he and Sandford had arrested. The address book was checked and, after some of the addresses had already been visited, officers called at the next one on the list, the *Claremont Hotel*, 95 Queen's Gate, Kensington. It was Thursday, 16 July 1959.

Given a detailed description of the wanted man, the hotel manager identified him as the man in room 15, a guest by the name of Paul Camay. Reinforcements were called for, and at 3.45pm, a number of officers assembled outside the door of room 15.

An officer hammered on the door, identified himself as a police officer and demanded that the door be opened. For a few seconds, all was silence, and then the police waiting outside heard a small click. This may well have been the wanted man turning the key in the lock, in order to admit the police, but equally, this man had already shot dead one police officer and that noise might have been the cocking of a gun. One of the more burly officers, Detective Sergeant Chambers, slammed into the door and knocked it flying. Unfortunately for the wanted man, he was immediately behind the door, crouching down to look through the keyhole, and got the full force of the blow in his face. Taken to St Stephen's Hospital, to receive treatment for his injury, the wanted man, known previously, as either Fisher or Levine, was shown to be Guenther Fritz Erwin Podola.

Guenther Podola had been born in Berlin on 8 February 1929. Growing up during the height of the Nazi era, Podola was in his early teens when his father was killed on the Russian front. Too young to fight himself, Podola was an active and fanatical member of the Hitler Youth.

After Germany's defeat, Podola found life in his own country very difficult and, in 1952, had emigrated to Canada, arriving there in the August of that year. He took a number of jobs, first in Quebec and later in Montreal, but he soon turned to a life of petty crime. In 1957, he received a short prison sentence for house-breaking. This was rapidly followed by a two-year term for eleven other offences. He was released on 25 July 1958, and deported back to Germany.

For a short time, Podola worked as a labourer in Stuttgart but on 21 May 1959, he had flown to London. Here he had turned back to petty crime, committing a number of burglaries, before his attempt to turn to blackmail after the Rowland Gardens robbery.

Held in the hospital, Podola claimed that he had lost his memory, and had no idea why the police had arrested him. Despite this claim, Podola was charged with the murder of Detective Sergeant Purdy, on 20 July.

Podola actually faced two trials. The first of these, on 10 September, was purely to decide if Podola's claim of memory loss were genuine or not. Various doctors were called. Some said that Podola could not possibly be faking, and his memory loss was genuine. Others testified that it was all a lie and he was pretending in order to avoid facing a murder trial. The deliberations took almost two weeks and it was not until 23 September that the jury returned their verdict: Podola was faking and knew perfectly well what crime he had committed. The following day, 24 September, the murder trial began.

Podola's trial for murder lasted for two days, before Mr Justice Davies. The case for the Crown was led by Mr Maxwell Turner, and Podola was defended by Mr Frederick Lawton. Asked how he wished to plead Podola persisted in his claim that he could not enter any plea as he had no memory of the crime for which he was being tried. The judge ordered that a not guilty plea be entered.

For the defence, Mr Lawton now suggested that the gun must have gone off accidentally and, therefore, his client was only guilty of manslaughter. This was disproved by Mr Nickolls of the Metropolitan Police Laboratory who had tested the weapon, and found it to be in perfect working order. It could not be fired accidentally, and required deliberate pressure on the trigger.

Having listened to all the evidence, the jury took just thirty-five minutes to decide that Podola was guilty, and he was then sentenced to death. Podola did not enter an appeal himself but, since the case had raised a difficult point of law, the Home Secretary referred the matter to the Court of Appeal himself.

The hearing took place on 15 October but it was decided that the verdict and sentence were safe.

Still every precaution was taken. A medical committee was established to examine Podola's mental condition. They decided, unanimously, that Podola's memory loss was a fake and that he had fully understood the case against him. Podola's last hope was lost on 2 November, when he was advised, through his solicitor, that the Home Secretary had found no grounds for interfering with the sentence of death.

Three days later, on Thursday, 5 November 1959, thirty-year-old Guenther Podola was hanged at Wandsworth prison by Harry Allen and Royston Rickard. He was the last man ever executed in Britain for the murder of a policeman.

Chapter 38

Marilyn Anne Bain
1962

ohn Michael Hubbard was growing rather tired of the noise from upstairs, at 60 Redcliffe Square. Almost every morning it seemed to be the same. Yesterday, the two women who lived upstairs had been screaming at each other at around 3.00am, and now, on Thursday, 13 September 1962, it was happening all over again.

Mr Hubbard, a solicitor, was first woken at about the same time, 3.00am, when the two women started arguing. He was unable to distinguish any of the words but the noise was constant for an hour or so. Finally, Mr Hubbard was able to drift off to sleep again, only to be woken for a second time, at 5.00am, by yet another argument. Though he was not to know it at the time, Mr Hubbard would only ever have his sleep disturbed, by the women upstairs, on one more occasion.

One of the women who lived in the flat upstairs was Marilyn Anne Bain. She had been born, in Fife, Scotland, on 21 March 1937. An intelligent girl, she did not, however, seem to excel at school but, once she had left, Marilyn had appeared to blossom somewhat. She joined the Army and served as a nurse in Hong Kong, Malaya, Singapore and at various locations within the United Kingdom.

In 1959, Marilyn was based in London. By now, she had realised that she had lesbian tendencies, and as part of her new life, often visited the Gateway Club, a well-known gathering place for gay people. It was there, in May 1959, that she first met Jean Doreen McVitie, who preferred to be known as Jeannette Blake. The two women got on famously, and Marilyn ended up spending ten days with Jean at her flat in Oakley Street, Chelsea.

The friendship between the two women soon became a love affair.

In September of that same year, 1959, Marilyn was discharged from the Army, with an excellent record. She immediately went to live with Jean, first at Oakley Street and later at Cremorne Mansions, also in Chelsea. After about a year there, the two lovers moved to Finborough Road, where they stayed for just two weeks, before moving to a basement flat at 16 Coleherne Road.

It was at that address that the physical relationship between Marilyn and Jean finally came to an end. One day, Marilyn met a man, who she knew only as Bob. They went out a few times and this led to tensions between her and Jean. At one stage Jean scathingly remarked that Marilyn must prefer men after all, but in fact, there was a deeper meaning to this argument.

The very early Sixties were not as enlightened as now, and many gay people still struggled with their own identities. Jean confessed to Marilyn, after another one of their arguments, that she wished she could be 'normal' like her friend, and seek the company of men. The two women talked through their problems and agreed that they would remain friends, and carry on living together, but their lesbian relationship was now over.

After about a year at Coleherne Road, the couple moved again, to the flat at 60 Redcliffe Square, Chelsea. Here, occasionally, despite the fact that she was not attracted to men, Jean would occasionally sleep with one in order to bring in some money. One such client visited the flat at some time between 8.30pm and 9.00pm, on the night of Thursday, 13 September 1962. When he had left, Jean had some extra money and she suggested to Marilyn that they should get some drinks in, and have a private party. Marilyn was all in favour and Jean then handed her £4, so that she could visit the off-licence.

Marilyn took the cash and went to the shop on the corner of Old Brompton Road and Earls Court Road. There she purchased a bottle of scotch whisky, a quarter bottle of brandy, three quarts of light ale, a bottle of ginger ale and five small bottles of cola to act as mixers. She then went back to the flat, where the two women began drinking heavily. By midnight, both were extremely drunk.

A game of ludo was suggested and played, but this was a little tame. Jean then suggested poker, but Marilyn did not know how to play. An hour or so passed with Jean teaching her friend the rudiments of poker, followed by a few games, and yet more drinks. Then, after one hand had finished, Jean got up to get some ice from the fridge.

Jean took a number of cubes out of the fridge and placed them onto a small blue plate, which she took back into the living room where Marilyn waited. Having dropped a cube into her own drink, Jean then dropped one into Marilyn's, She, however, did not want ice so she took the cube out and dropped it back onto the plate. It was that simple event which led to a new argument, ending with the playing cards being thrown up into the air.

The cards were now all over the floor and yet another argument followed over who should pick them up. Eventually, it was Jean who collected the cards together, and the two women then sat in silence for a while, angry with each other. In due course, that anger boiled over into yet another heated discussion, ending in a physical fight between the two. Punches were exchanged and the fight only stopped when Jean slid to the ground, and Marilyn went to the toilet to be sick.

Going back into the living room, Marilyn saw, to her horror, that Jean was slumped on the floor, an ever-widening pool of blood seeping through her blouse. Though she was still quite drunk, Marilyn realised that something was wrong. She immediately ran off to find a telephone and ring for an ambulance.

Harry Sidney Fox was the driver of the ambulance sent to Redcliffe Square. He timed his arrival at 8.20am on the morning of 14 September. As he pulled his vehicle into the street, he saw Marilyn Bain waiting outside, frantically waving to attract his attention. She shouted, 'Come in the house quickly. My friend has collapsed on the floor.' Going into the flat, Fox found Jean lying near the sideboard, her head resting on a pillow. It was clear that she had been stabbed, though there was no sign of a knife anywhere in the room. Both the injured woman, and her friend, were taken to the Princess Beatrice Hospital. On the way, Jean remarked, 'She knifed me.' She then paused for a few seconds before adding, 'She doesn't know anything about it.'

In a case of stabbing, the police are, obviously, informed that an incident has taken place. The hospital duly contacted them and, at 8.45am, Detective Sergeant Edward Smith and Detective Sergeant Alan Busby, attended the hospital to investigate. Jean was still being treated for her injury, but Smith did speak to Marilyn. He began by saying, 'I understand a friend of yours has been stabbed.' To this, Marilyn replied, 'I don't know what happened. I saw her in the room. She was holding her chest and she said she couldn't breathe. I rushed out and phoned for an ambulance.'

After some time, Sergeant Smith was informed that Jean was able to make a statement. Having heard her side of the story, he then returned to Marilyn and said, 'Miss Blake says you stabbed her. What happened?' Marilyn replied, 'I can't remember. We had been drinking all night and we always fight.' She was then taken to Chelsea police station where she was charged with wounding and released on police bail, having been told to return to the station at 2.00pm the next day.

The following day, when Marilyn did return to the police station, she was given some good news. By now, Jean had been interviewed again, and she had made it clear that she did not wish to press charges against her friend. The charges were now dropped and Marilyn was free to go. It was not, however, the end of her problems, for the next day, Monday, 17 September, Marilyn received a visit from a policeman, at her home.

That officer was Chief Inspector Lansdall and he informed Marilyn that Jean had now died, and that she might now be charged with a serious offence. First, there would have to be a post-mortem, and if that showed that Jean had died as a direct result of the stab wound, then Marilyn would be facing a charge of murder. In the meantime, she was to return to Chelsea police station in order to make a full written statement.

Marilyn made no attempt to hide what she had done. In fact,

she actively helped the police in their enquiries. Before she left the flat to go back to the police station, Marilyn said that she had been tidying the flat and had found the knife she had used, underneath the fridge. It must have fallen there, or perhaps been knocked under there, in the struggle with Jean. Chief Inspector Lansdall could not help but notice the dried blood on the knife. Marilyn had made no attempt to clean it or wipe away any of the evidence against her.

Whilst Marilyn was at the station, news came through that a preliminary post-mortem had shown that the stab wound was the direct cause of death. Dr Robert Donald Teare had noted a single stab wound on the left side of the chest, at an angle of twenty-five degrees to the horizontal. That stab had gone through between the sixth and seventh rib, into the diaphragm, through the top of the stomach and into the centre of the chest. The wound was five inches deep, but would only have required light to moderate force to inflict, as the flesh there was easily penetrated. Indeed, the wound might well have been caused by Jean falling onto the knife, accidentally, during the fight. The track of the wound had since become infected and it was that, which had led to Jean's death.

Marilyn was then charged with murder. When the case came to trial, however, it was clear that this had all been a tragic accident. Mr Sebag Shaw, for the defence, said that his client pleaded not guilty to murder but would plead guilty to manslaughter. After a brief discussion, that plea was accepted and the murder charge was not proceeded with. It remained only to detail any previous convictions against Marilyn. There was only one. On 20 April 1960, at the West London Metropolitan Magistrates' Court, she had been given eighteen months' probation for stealing two wing mirrors from a car.

Marilyn Anne Bain, a woman who deeply regretted that she had taken the life of her friend, was then sentenced to three years' imprisonment.

Chapter 39

Robert Lipman
1967

Mark Trevelyan Victor Shaw-Lawrence ran his tour operator's business from offices on the first floor of 17 Walpole Street, Chelsea. In fact, Mark owned the entire building and rented out rooms and flats on the other floors to various tenants.

Amongst those tenants was a young nineteen-year-old French woman who occupied flat 6, which consisted of two rooms on the third floor, Claudie Delbarre, who was better known as Claudie Daniels.

The block at Walpole Street had a public pay-phone, in the hallway, just outside Mark's offices and it was common practice for the tenants to receive calls on that number. Someone from the office would usually answer the telephone and then dash to the appropriate tenant and tell them that they had a call. So it was that when someone rang for Miss Delbarre, at around 10.30am on Tuesday, 19 September 1967, a Miss Sparke-Davies was despatched to tell Claudie that someone wished to speak to her. Unfortunately, Miss Delbarre did not appear to be at home, as there was no reply to Miss Sparke-Davies's knocking on her flat door.

At 11.45am, another call came through for Claudie Delbarre but, again, she did not seem to be at home. Soon after this, another of the tenants, Keith Money, who lived in the ground floor flat, called in at the office and happened to remark that he hadn't seen Claudie since Saturday, 16 September. This was most unusual. Claudie was a girl fond of parties, going out and visiting friends and it was very strange that she had not been seen for more than three days. Mark Shaw-Lawrence felt that perhaps Claudie might be ill so, taking his master key, he and Keith went up to her rooms to investigate.

Opening the front door of the flat, Mark called out for Claudie, but still there was no reply. Going into the bedroom he saw a figure lying in the bed and, assuming Claudie was asleep, called out to her again, but still there was no reply, and no sign of movement. Walking forward tentatively, Mark pulled back the bedsheet a little, to find Claudie lying in bed, almost naked. There was obviously something very wrong here, so Mark locked up the flat again and decided to send for a doctor.

The nearest surgery was not far away and a member of staff was sent to fetch the doctor. It transpired that the usual doctor was on holiday, and the surgery was being manned by a locum, a Dr Davidson. Details of what Mark had found were given to the receptionist, who said she would pass the information on to Dr Davidson. The doctor, however, did not attend. A second visit to the surgery was made, but it was not until the third visit that Dr Davidson admitted that he was refusing to visit the flat, as he did not wish to get involved. He advised Mark to contact the police instead. This rather callous delay meant that it was not until 12.25pm, that the police were contacted.

The police did not delay and, at 12.28pm, Constable Michael Argent arrived at 17 Walpole Street. Going up to flat number 6, he viewed the body himself before calling in the police surgeon, Dr Albert Lovell.

At 12.45pm, Dr Lovell arrived. He confirmed that life was extinct and noticed that the bed appeared to have pulled away from the wall a little. There was a triangular-shaped gap between the bed and the wall and in this area, Dr Lovell noticed a broken glass. It was also clear that someone else must have been inside the flat. There were a great number of cigarette stubs, of two different types, in the ashtray, and two cups which were half full of cold tea. Dr Lovell also found fifteen Flagyl tablets on a mantle shelf and six tablets of Tetracycline in the sitting room. More importantly, perhaps, Dr Lovell noticed that Claudie's mouth had been stuffed with some material from the bed. There were also some small bruises on her body; one near her jaw on the right and two more on her forearm. This did not look like a straightforward case and Dr Lovell advised Constable Argent to contact his station and report the matter to CID.

The officers conducting the investigation, collected the broken pieces of glass from the side of the bed and dusted them for fingerprints. One set was found and these did not match the prints taken from the dead woman, indicating that they, most likely, belonged to whoever had been in the flat with her. The same prints were found on one of the tea cups, and at other locations around the flat. When those prints were checked against the police database, a name was revealed. The prints belonged to a man named Robert Lipman.

Lipman was an American, who lived in New York, but he was a regular visitor to Britain and, quite recently, he had been arrested for being in possession of cannabis resin on 11 September 1967, and had been fined £25. This in turn meant that the police not only had his fingerprints, but also a detailed description: six feet six inches tall, heavy build, dark brown hair with grey streaks. They also knew that he was the holder of American passport number F 86.2012 and an international driving licence numbered 256776; and even that he had been born in New York city on 21 July 1931.

It was a simple matter to trace the hotel where Lipman was staying at. Checks showed that he had arrived in Britain on Monday, 11 September, the day he had been arrested, and had travelled to the *Knightsbridge Green Hotel*, at 159 Knightsbridge. The police duly visited the hotel, where they spoke to the receptionist, Mercia Jane de Baeupre-Tapping. Mercia confirmed that Lipman had arrived at the hotel at some time between 11.00am and 12.30pm on 11 September, and had asked for a single suite, saying that he intended staying for a couple of weeks. He was given room 5.

Exactly one week later, on Monday, 18 September, Mercia had been on duty at the front desk, when she saw Lipman rush in from outside. He was wearing a blue jacket, grey trousers and a light shirt, but no tie. His hair was dishevelled and he appeared not to have either washed or shaved. He asked if there were any messages for him and, told that they were not, ran up the stairs to his room. Just five minutes later he rang down and said he wanted his bill drawn up as he was leaving immediately.

At 9.40am, Lipman was back downstairs, asking for his bill, which Mercia was still in the process of making up. Lipman had still not washed or shaved and seemed to be in a great hurry. He was very agitated and at one stage shouted, 'Quick, quick, where's my bill.' Mercia told him she was still making it up and he replied, 'I don't care, just let me know how much I owe and I'll write out a cheque.'

Mercia pointed out that it was hotel policy not to accept cheques, whereupon Lipman became very angry. Eventually, Mercia had to speak to the manager, who agreed to take a cheque this time. Lipman scribbled out one for £12 19s 6d and then ran from the hotel.

The police now had to find where Lipman had run to. It seemed reasonable to assume that if he were connected with Claudie's death in some way, and had been in such a hurry to check out of his hotel, then he might well be trying to leave the country. Local travel agents were interviewed and this led officers to call on Brian Frederick Andrews, a ticket agent who operated a company named Cedars Travel, from offices at 18e Curzon Street.

Brian confirmed that at around 10.00am on 18 September, Lipman had come into the office asking about flights to Lisbon that morning. Lipman was given the times and the prices of the various flights available, but then changed his mind and said he wished to fly to Copenhagen instead. He explained that his ex-wife lived there and he could visit her first, before getting a flight from there to Lisbon, in a few days time. After some further discussion, a flight leaving at 12.40pm was booked, at a price of £78 13s. Once again, Robert Lipman paid by cheque, before the receptionist rang for a cab to take him to the airport.

That cab driver, Dennis Murphy, was traced, and he told police that he had been called to the travel agents at 11.00am on 18 September. He saw a very tall, well-built man waiting outside and asked if he were Mr Lipman. Once Lipman had confirmed that he was the fare, Murphy got out to put the luggage into his cab. Lipman was in such a hurry that he helped Murphy, and at one stage, whilst collecting his bag from inside the travel agents, knocked over a silver metallic vase. Flowers and water went all over the floor but Lipman did not stop to help clear the mess up.

Having heard Lipman's American accent, Murphy assumed that his fare was travelling to the United States and so took him to the wrong terminal. Lipman was furious, but was finally taken to the correct area. Murphy dropped him off at 12.15pm. There could now be no doubt; Lipman had escaped, the day before Claudie Delbarre's body had been found.

The matter was not left to rest there. Lipman may well have escaped to Copenhagen and would probably move on to Lisbon from there, but eventually he would return to his native country, and his home city of New York. The British police now contacted their American counterparts and the extradition process was started. It was this which eventually led to two officers, Detective Superintendent Huntley and Detective Chief Inspector Fred Lambert to fly to Kennedy airport on 30 April 1968. There, at 7.00pm, they took charge of Robert Lipman, and then all three men flew back to England. At 10.05pm, on 1 May, Lipman was charged with murder at the Chelsea police station.

Lipman's trial took place at the Old Bailey on 10 October 1968, before Mr Justice Milmo. The case for the prosecution was led by Mr John Mathew, assisted by Mr Brian Leary. Lipman was defended by Mr Michael Eastham and Mr Norman King.

Witnesses were called to detail the movements of both Lipman and Claudie Delbarre on Saturday, 16 September, the last day she had been seen alive, and the day she had first met Robert Lipman.

Stephen Richard Saunders was an American, who had moved to London on 23 December 1966, and now lived at 1 Oakley Gardens. He testified that he had been invited to a meal at the Bagdad Restaurant, by Benny Carruthers, an actor he knew. They had arrived at the restaurant at about 10.40pm on 16

September, where they had met some people they knew, and others, who were friends of friends. Saunders said that already present were Maggie Foote, her sister, Judy Foote, Ian Quarrier, a woman named Paula and two others; Bob Lipman and Claudie. Stephen had also taken along his girlfriend, Shay Davidson.

The group all enjoyed a meal together, finally leaving at some time between 12.30am and 12.45am on Sunday, 17 September. The party separated after the meal, all going their different ways, in smaller groups, but they all agreed to meet up later, at a club called the *Speak Easy*, at 48 Margaret Street. First, however, Stephen dropped Lipman off at his hotel, as he wanted to change his clothes.

In due course, everyone met at the *Speak Easy*, where they all had a few drinks. When Stephen left, he gave a lift to four people: Shay Davidson, Maggie Foote, Robert Lipman and Claudie Delbarre. The first people he dropped off were Lipman and Claudie, who asked to get out at the Sloane Square cab rank. It was then some time after 4.00am.

That was the last time that anyone saw Lipman and Claudie together. It seemed reasonable to assume that he had then gone back to her flat, where she had been killed and Robert had then rushed back to his hotel, packed his belongings, booked a flight and ultimately left the country.

Details of the cause of Claudie's death were given by Professor Donald Teare who had performed the post-mortem. He described Claudie as a young girl, five feet one inches tall in life. The bruises on her body had occurred just before she died and it seemed clear that she had been struck on the head, by the glass, which had shattered and fallen to the floor by the bed. This blow would have rendered Claudie unconscious and eventually lead to a cerebral haemorrhage. However, the direct cause of death was suffocation, due to the material stuffed into Claudie's mouth.

Lipman did step into the witness box to give his own version of the events that took place inside Claudie's flat on that fateful day. He claimed that both he and Claudie had taken LSD and he had then had a 'bad trip'. He had the illusion that he was descending to the centre of the earth and, once there, he was attacked by large snakes. He had tried to fight these snakes off and he must have struck Claudie, accidentally, during this time. When he woke up later he found her dead in the bed, panicked and fled the country.

The jury retired to consider their verdict and, after some time, sent a note to the judge asking for guidance as they could not agree on a unanimous verdict. Eventually, after receiving that guidance, they found Lipman not guilty of murder, but guilty of manslaughter. Even then they could not agree and had to return a majority verdict of ten to two. Lipman was then sentenced to serve six years in prison and, once free, would be deported.

On 28 July 1969, Lipman appealed against his conviction and his sentence. The case was heard by Lord Justice Widgery, Lord Justice Atkinson, and Mr Justice James. After three days of hearing evidence and deliberating the various legal arguments, they ruled that the conviction was safe and the sentence of six years must stand.

In fact, Robert Lipman, as is usual, did not serve the full six years. Having obtained the statutory remission, he was freed in early 1971. On 1 February of that year, he was deported back to the United States.

Chapter 40

Other Murders and Foul Deeds
Various Dates

n addition to the crimes mentioned in the previous chapters of this book, other murders and foul deeds took place within the confines of Chelsea and Kensington. These stories are covered here in chronological order.

(1) Fanny Young, 1863

Fanny, who was not yet nineteen years of age, was in service to Arthur Buller and his family, in Kensington. She had worked for them for eight months and was highly regarded by the family.

As Fanny's stay progressed, the family could not help but notice that Fanny appeared to be putting on a good deal of weight. More specifically, that weight seemed to be concentrated around the stomach region but, when questioned, she denied that she was pregnant.

One day in November, Fanny's new weight suddenly vanished overnight. Suspicious of this, the family made a search of the house and, in a drawer in Fanny's bedroom, the body of a child was discovered, wrapped in a napkin.

At both the subsequent magistrates' court and the coroner's court, Fanny was found guilty of murder. However, the Grand Jury overturned both verdicts and when Fanny appeared at the Old Bailey, before Mr Justice Blackburn, on 14 December, the charge had been reduced to one of concealing the birth of her illegitimate child. Originally she pleaded not guilty but her counsel, Mr Ribton, informed the judge that he was unable to argue against the charge. It was tantamount to the defence council saying that his client was guilty. After some discussion, Fanny changed her plea to guilty whereupon sentence was deferred until the next session of the court. Eventually, Fanny was to escape prison altogether, the State believing that she had already suffered enough.

(2) The murder of Mary Ann Walsh, 1881

Mary's body was found in the front garden of 162 King's Road, Chelsea on a Wednesday in mid-February, 1881. There were signs that she had been strangled.

A subsequent post-mortem examination by Dr Pearce of Markham Square showed that there were finger marks on Mary's neck, and she had also been struck a number of times about the head and shoulders, but the direct cause of death was exposure. She had been attacked on a particularly cold night, rendered unconscious and left to die in the cold. It was, nevertheless, a case of murder.

The inquest was held at the *Hope Tavern*, in Arthur Street, Chelsea, before Dr Diplock. As expected, the verdict was 'murder by person or persons unknown'.

(3) The murder of Ernest Castelein, 1945

Ernest Castelein was a native of Belgium and quite an accomplished artist. He had exhibited in his own country and now operated from a studio in Cromwell Road, Kensington.

On Wednesday, 25 July 1945, a nurse walking past the studio heard a deep groaning. She telephoned the police who broke into the building and found Ernest lying on the floor. He had been badly beaten and was rushed to hospital in Wimbledon. Ernest never recovered consciousness and died from his injuries on Monday, 30 July.

A thorough police investigation by Scotland Yard included speaking to all taxi-drivers, who may have picked up a fare early on the morning of 25 July. This led to a description of a tall man, who had been seen in the vicinity of Gloucester Road and Cromwell Road in the early hours of that Wednesday. Unfortunately, witnesses were unable to say whether or not the man had been a soldier or a civilian and, with so little to go on, the investigation soon ran out of steam. The attacker was never traced and the murder remains unsolved.

(4) The murder of Violet McGrath, 1954

On the morning of Sunday, 9 May 1954, the body of sixty-four-year-old Violet McGrath was found in her flat in Onslow Square, Kensington. She had been battered and strangled to death, and a trail of blood led from behind the front door, implying that was where the attack had started. It also suggested that the killer may well have been known to Violet and that she had been attacked, as she was letting him out of the flat.

A neighbour told police that he had heard a dull thud coming from next door, at about noon, which narrowed down the time of the attack, but no witness could be found who had seen anyone leaving the house at that time, or shortly afterwards.

A possible motive for the crime was soon discovered. A couple of days before she had died, Violet had withdrawn a large amount of cash, and no trace of this was found inside her home, suggesting that robbery may have been the motive.

Despite the fact that when her body was found, Violet was lying next to a magazine containing an article on fingerprints, no trace of her killer was ever found.

(5) The murder of Countess Teresa Lubienska, 1957

Teresa Lubienska was a war heroine. She had been held in Ravensbruck concentration camp, where she tried her best to comfort her fellow prisoners. For that reason she was given the nickname the Angel of Ravensbruck.

On the night of 24 May 1957, Teresa went to a friend's house in Ealing, for a meal. Leaving late at night, to return to her house in Cornwall Gardens, she was accompanied onto the underground by a Catholic priest, who had also been at the meal. The priest alighted at Earl's Court. Teresa travelled on to Gloucester Road station, where she got off the train at 10.19pm. Minutes later, Teresa staggered into the lift, bleeding badly from five stab wounds in her chest. She was only able to shout, 'Bandits! Bandits!'

Teresa died from her wounds in the ambulance taking her to hospital. Some sources have suggested that she was merely the victim of a mugging but that is unlikely as her handbag was found in the lift, and she still wore a valuable brooch on her lapel. Perhaps a better suggestion is that she was deliberately targeted, as she had been a vociferous opponent of the communist Polish government.

The investigation into Teresa's death lasted for more than four years and thousands of statements were taken. None of it ever brought the police closer to arresting the culprit.

(6) Archibald Thompson Hall, 1977

Archibald Hall, who also used the alias Roy Fontaine, was a butler, with a lucrative sideline in theft. Hall's routine was to take a position in a high-class household, usually forging his own references in order to obtain employment, and then steal what he could before moving on. He was also adept at forging signatures and often used that skill to take money from his employer's bank accounts. This life of crime led to various prison sentences but, upon his release, Hall would always return to his criminal ways.

In November 1977, Hall obtained a position as butler to a retired Labour member of parliament, Walter Scott-Elliott and his wife, Dorothy, at their flat at 22 Richmond Court, Sloane Street, Kensington. The Scott-Elliott's were an extremely rich family with houses in France and Italy. Their London home was crammed with valuable antiques and collectibles and Hall decided that they were perfect targets. Walter was, by this time, rather senile and his wife was suffering from acute arthritis.

In order to steal as much as possible, Hall decided he needed some assistance. He contacted an old ex-girlfriend, Mary Coggle and she, in turn, suggested a friend of hers, a petty crook named Michael Kitto. The three decided to work together to steal as much as possible from the Scott-Elliotts.

In December 1977, Dorothy Scott-Elliott spent some time in hospital. This was the perfect time to rob the flat and, on 8 December, Hall invited Kitto into the flat to determine what they would take. As Kitto was being taken on his conducted tour, he and Hall walked into Dorothy Scott-Elliott's bedroom. Unfortunately for them, she had been released early from hospital, and demanded to know what they were doing in her room. Hall silenced her by smothering her with a pillow.

Walter Scott-Elliott was in his own bedroom and shouted out, asking what the commotion was. Hall went into his room, told him that his wife had been having a nightmare, but was now fine. Walter accepted this and went back to sleep.

Dorothy's body had to be disposed of, but Walter couldn't be left in the house by himself. The solution was to engage the services of Mary Coggle, who dressed up as Dorothy and wore a wig and the dead woman's fur coat. Dorothy's body was then placed into the boot of the family car and Hall then drove it up to Scotland. Walter was drugged and didn't even realise that the woman sitting in the car next to him was not in fact his wife.

Near Loch Earn, Dorothy's body was thrown into a stream. Hall then drove Walter to a hideout in Cumbria, before he and Kitto returned to Sloane Street, and ransacked the flat. They then returned to Cumbria, collected Walter, took him back to Scotland and strangled him. When he did not die immediately, Hall battered him to death using a spade. His body was then buried in a shallow grave.

Hall's problems were still not over, however. Mary Coggle had taken a liking to Dorothy's fur coats and insisted on keeping them for herself. Hall and Kitto wished to sell them. The solution was obvious. Mary was smothered to death with a plastic bag and her body thrown into a stream.

Still the murders were not at an end. Over Christmas, Hall and Kitto stayed with Hall's brother, Donald. After enjoying his hospitality, Hall killed his brother mainly because, as he was to say later, he had never really liked him.

Once again, the plan was to dispose of Donald Hall's body in Scotland. On the way north, Hall and Kitto stayed at a hotel in North Berwick, where they changed the number plates on their car, just in case any potential witnesses should spot them driving north. Unfortunately, on the way to dispose of the body, Hall and Kitto were stopped at a routine police checkpoint, where it was revealed that the number plates did not match the make of car.

Arrested, Hall made a full confession to the police, also admitting an earlier murder where he had killed an associate and buried his body in the bed of a stream in Scotland. In all, he was now admitting to five murders, two in Scotland, two in Cumbria and one in Kensington. Tried in Edinburgh, both Hall and Kitto were sentenced to life imprisonment.

Index